KALE, GLORIOUS KALE

CATHERINE WALTHERS
Photographs by Alison Shaw

The Countryman Press
Woodstock, Vermont

Book design and composition by Vicky Vaughn Shea, Ponderosa Pine Design

Library of Congress Cataloging-in-Publication Data are available.
Kale, Glorious Kale
978-58157-245-2

Published by The Countryman Press, P.O. Box 748, Woodstock, VT 05091
Distributed by W. W. Norton & Company, Inc., 500 Fifth Avenue, New York, NY 10110
Printed in the United States of America

10 9 8 7 6 5 4 3 2 1

For James and David Kelliher, my nightly dinner companions

Contents

Introduction

Even after 140 days straight of eating kale, I hadn't had enough. Give or take one or two days, I ate kale—with my family—at one or more meals every day for five months. And a few times, kale was part of every meal of the day—breakfast, lunch and dinner.

If anything, my appreciation for this green grew. When it came time for my deadline, I wanted to keep going. I still had ideas to test. What about the kale and corn chowder I had once made but not retested? And the polenta topped with mushrooms and kale that I had liked but not recorded? The very day I was writing this introduction, a friend who was using my commercial kitchen out back came over with dish of polenta topped with caramelized onions, sausage, white beans and sautéed baby kale. Coincidental?

And I was still getting calls. Experimenting on their own with kale, friends and others were letting me know when they had made something good. One had just served lamb meatballs over thinly sliced sautéed kale, using kale as a replacement for pasta. A great idea. Another suggested adding crispy kale to the top of commercial pizza. Still another friend paired kale with shrimp, chipotle peppers, avocado and lime in a tortilla soup. Her family raved. Luckily I had time to re-create this, and it became the eleventh recipe in the kale soup chapter.

Kale, it turns out, is amazingly versatile and easy to enjoy, as I hope each and every one of you will find out, if you haven't already. We enjoyed a cocktails and kale evening; a Greek kale night and kale pizza night. At one point, my husband said, "We should call this book *One Thousand Ways to Hide Kale*." Only I wasn't trying to hide it. Kale has a natural affinity to many, many ingredients.

Some novelists say they follow the lead of the characters they've created to let them reveal the story. I felt like that with kale. Although I knew quite a bit about kale when I started the project, I was open to where it would take me.

After all, I had taught dozens of classes on the subject and organized an entire festival dedicated to kale. I'd written a cookbook on greens—with a chapter on kale—some years before the invention of kale chips or kale smoothies. Why didn't I foresee those blockbusters? What would come next?

There were happy surprises. Baby kale, for one. It looks like more mature kale, only in miniature, tender and tasty. Now farmers are bagging it like baby lettuce or arugula. Baby kale salads were being rolled out of my kitchen like candy on a conveyer belt.

I started growing baby kale in the garden—in October—and I wholeheartedly recommend this. It grew, I cut it with scissors for a salad; it grew back. Again and again. Even after a December snowstorm in Massachusetts, I kicked off some snow and there it was, bright green kale happily hanging out in the garden, ready for use.

When all else is gone for the growing season, there's still kale. It's surprising that it didn't become a superstar even earlier.

The uses for massaged kale were another surprise. Massaging kale is the very effective method of rubbing olive oil and salt to tenderize raw kale for a salad. Massaged kale can also go on pizzas, in burgers, in meat loaf.

Massaged kale is also perfect in combination with grains and beans. It can hold its own and doesn't wilt—kale and quinoa salad; Greek kale and farro; stir-fried rice with kale; kale veggie burgers. Even with the emergence of baby kale for salads, there was still plenty of room for massaged kale.

I had been enjoying crispy kale for a few years, but could there be more? Crispy kale and granola has become my absolute favorite breakfast snack. And kale, bacon and pumpkin crunch is addictive (kale crack, my friend called it).

Kale can also be roasted as a side dish. It's great with roasted cauliflower, or roasted carrots and parsnips. Grilling is another surprisingly easy way to prepare kale—as simple as throwing on a few oiled leaves on the grill for a minute or two. Try this in a kale panzanella salad with grilled bread and juicy summer tomatoes.

And so it went. Ninety recipes later, kale proved its superstar status. The nutritional research pointing to kale as the top most nutritious vegetable only confirms this. The Center for Science in the Public Interest ranked kale number one in a nutrition comparison with 83 other vegetables. And in the Aggregate Nutrient Density Index (ANDI for short) used at Whole Foods Market, where plant-based foods are ranked on a scale of 0 to 1,000, kale came in at 1,000.

No wonder I felt great, as a side effect of writing this book. I had so much energy. And eating so much kale every day left little room for snacks or junk. Any extra weight I had slipped away. I became convinced, more than ever, that eating healthy every day is key, not dieting.

All Hail to Kale!

THE KALE CHRONICLES

I kept a journal of each day of writing the book, and called the file "The Kale Chronicles." I noted the recipes created and tested each day, and general comments and thoughts. Certain themes emerge throughout—and the kale testing weaves between family, community, art and eating. A few of those stories are included here, throughout the book.

I hope your experiences with kale, and knowledge thereof, are elevated through this work. But my fondest hope would be for enjoyable cooking experiences as well as memorable meals with your family and friends.

RED CHIDORI

WINTERBOR

WINTER RED

SPIGARIELLO
LISCIA

RED RUSSIAN

WHITE RUSSIAN

RED URSA

TOSCANNO

BLUE SCOTCH

THE KALE CHRONICLES

The Glorious Varieties of Kale

If you think you're confused now about what variety of kale to buy, get ready to have your head spin.

Seed Savers lists fifty varieties, from Bare Necessities kale, sweet and crunchy, to Wild Red, a variation of a Siberian kale. And such farmers as Rusty Gordon are growing more and more different kale types.

Rusty grew 13 kinds last year at his Ghost Island Farm on Martha's Vineyard.

Why?

"I don't know," Rusty shrugs. Fortunately, he says, his fascination with kale has coincided with a public surge in interest.

"Just three years ago it seemed like no one was interested in kale. I couldn't sell it in the spring or summer," he explains. Fall was his big season, especially on the Vineyard, where it's traditionally used for Portuguese kale soup with sausage, potato and beans. "I'm just lucky it's this big thing now."

His favorite variety: Beira, a specialty kale from Portugal that has wider, flatter leaves, more like a collard green. Beira is the traditional leaf kale for Portuguese kale soup.

Beira is available from Johnny's Selected Seeds, an employee-owned seed company based in Maine that has approximately eight kale varieties for sale—if it can be kept in stock, due to a surge in popularity with kale.

Johnny's most popular kale variety in 2012, Winterbor, was unavailable for purchase more recently. "Unfortunately, that was our number one selling variety," reports Paul Gallione, a spokesperson for Johnny's. The company's second-most-popular variety, Toscano, the Italian heirloom nicknamed "dinosaur kale" for its crinkly leaves, was also not available this year. The organic variety had a crop failure, limiting seed supply.

According to Gallione, this overall interest in kale has led to a worldwide shortage of kale seeds. "It's been brought on by a couple of factors; the most important has been the exponential growth in kale," he says. "It's been touted by certain people as the new superfood, so that puts stress on the supply." In addition, Gallione says, it takes eighteen to twenty months—nearly two years—to produce seed from kale.

But let's back up here, because there is a fairly easy way to categorize kale. Generally, we see three standard kale types in supermarkets: the curly kales, Russian kales and Italian crinkly kales.

Of these, the dark blue-green, curly kales came first. These kales originated in Europe, and are often referred to as the Scotch kales. Kale was one of the most common green vegetables eaten in Europe up until the end of the Middle Ages. Although the larger ruffled leaves appear the most formidable to people, cooked properly, curly kale is tender and pleasant tasting, not bitter. In seed catalogs, you see the incarnations of this kale: the standard Winterbor; Ripbor, similar with slightly more ruffles; and Starbor, with tight curls.

Redbor, a striking magenta version of the curly kale, is now being grown and sold at farmers' markets.

Johanna Finley of Finley Farms in California finds the Redbor a new favorite for raw kale salad. "It tends to be sweeter and slightly more tender, and it's so beautiful, being purple," says Johanna. "It's a very nice presentation. Anything you put in it, like cranberries or toasted nuts, really stands out."

On the East Coast, Beedy's Camden is a newer variety of curly kale carried by Fedco Seeds, also located in Maine. It's named after Beedy Parker, a member of the Maine Organic Farmers and Gardeners Association, who explains she found it growing in her Maine garden, probably from nature's own selective breeding. It's not as tightly ruffled as Winterbor; the wavy leaves are full to the bottom of each stalk.

Beedy says she took notice of the kale, how long into the winter it continued to grow as well as its tenderness and flavor. She would save the seeds and share them with friends. She eventually sent seeds to a few seed companies and Fedco ended up growing it and carrying it. Fedco says at one point it stopped carrying Beedy's Camden, but then brought it back because of customer demand.

In the late nineties, we began to see Red Russian kale in markets, though many of these heirlooms have been around for decades. Red Russian leaves are a flatter than the curly kale, with a noticeable web of purple veins (which turn green when cooked) and ragged rather than curly edges. Although in the same family as other kales, the Red Russian and Siberian kales are a different species, *Brassica napus* var. *pabularia*, with a different leaf structure.

The Red Russian and Siberian kales originate, as the names imply, from northern Europe and northern Asia, and a number of these seeds have been traced to Russian traders' coming to Canada in the late 1880s. Red Russian kale has even been nicknamed "Communist Kale" by some farmworkers in Maine.

As with most all kale varieties, if you grow them in your garden, the plants live through the fall, and the flavor gets sweeter after a frost. Russian kale leaves are among the most tender of the traditional kales, with a mild, sweet flavor. These greens melt down quite a bit in a sauté pan, and are used often in raw salads.

White Russian kale, a silvery green kale with white veining, is now becoming available in markets. A beautiful Siberian kale is available through Johnny's Selected Seeds, and it is described as "more tender than the extra curly varieties."

This was developed by Frank Morton, a farmer and kale breeder who owns Wild Garden Seed Co. in Philomath, Oregon. White Russian, says Morton, is an open-pollinated cross between Red Russian kale and Siberian. He has been told by a number of chefs it is their favorite kale.

Another variety that he bred at his Gathering Together Farm and sells is Red Ursa, which also combines the broad frills of Siberian kale with the color of Red Russian. Red Ursa, he explains tastes like kale should taste. The texture is very meaty; the leaves are thick, more like a Siberian. The ruffliness creates a texture in your mouth. The mid rib is pretty large and sweet—there's a lot of sugar in the stem, he notes.

When this variety was included in the national gardening trials in 1997, Morton reports, it was selected as one of the top five new vegetable introductions that year, and describes it as very sweet, colorful and with a great raw flavor for salads.

Some more obscure cousins of Red Russian kale—Russian Blue, Russian Mike, Ragged Jack, Russian Hunger and Russian Frills, a Red Russian kale type with "frills upon frills upon frills"—may or may not come to market. These heirlooms are being grown and saved by members of Seed Savers, an organization in which members collect, grow and share heirloom and open-pollinated seeds.

Other heirloom kale—varieties handed down from one generation to another—came to the United States through immigrants who brought favorite plant seeds with them, and are being kept alive by Seed Saver growers. Smooth German kale, sweet and tender with good flavor, for example, is being grown by Irene Kemper in Walton, Maine. Her great-grandparents brought the seeds here from Germany.

A Sutherland kale, another heirloom, is described as a "true Scottish" kale that doesn't need a frost to be tender. Another variety known as Crispy Blue originates from China, where it is known as *gai-lan*. This kale has glossy blue leaves and flower buds similar to broccoli rabe, and tastes like a cross between broccoli and kale, with a "small hint of agreeable bitterness and sweetness."

The heirloom kales from Italy sold as Tuscan, Toscano and lacinato kale, are the newest to the market over the last decade, but have quickly become one of the most popular types of kale. They have distinctive straplike leaves, very dark green and crinkled, which led to the nickname "dinosaur kale." This can be a very tender kale green with a mild kale flavor, melting away in soups and sautés. It can work nicely raw in salads, but at other times, can be too tough for this, depending on the growing conditions more so than the variety.

In gardens and fields, these Italian heirlooms look like miniature palm trees, especially as the plant grows throughout the season and leaves are picked from the bottom. Other Italian kales in this collection are Cavolo Nero (Tuscan Black or Nero di Tuscana), as the leaves can appear black from a distance.

Rainbow lacinato kale is now on the market. It's a cross between lacinato and Redbor: it looks like dinosaur kale overlaid with reds, blues and purples. This kale also came from Oregon farmer Frank Morton.

"I wanted a purple lacinato," Morton says. He loved the good flavor of the lacinato kale, but also hoped to give it a bit of color from Redbor, a hybrid, which in his opinion, doesn't have a lot of flavor, but a stunning color with some other good growing qualities, such as a strong stem and disease resistance.

KALE TYPES AT A GLANCE

Although there are many more varieties of kale at the market and available to grow, there is no reason to worry about what is the best kind to cook with or use in salads. Instead, look at their broad range as an opportunity to experiment and be adventurous.

As someone who has been testing kale and developing recipes for years, I find most of the kale varieties interchangeable on the whole. In other words, generally you won't go wrong buying one type over the other.

Rarely do I distinguish which type of kale to use in a particular recipe, so you can take that as a signal to use whatever variety you have. When I do, I usually mention a particular reason, such as to use a Red Russian kale or lacinato kale, which cooks down more in volume than do curly kales.

In appearance—ruffles, color, shapes—kales can look quite different. But in terms of taste, while there are differences, I'd say these are subtle. Some kales are more tender than others, but all types can be tender.

What can sometimes be more important is how the kale was grown and cared for—did it get enough water, was it attacked by insects? Environmentally stressed kale plants don't taste as good, so it is important to try different farms or markets until you find your favorite growers. Kale, as a whole, is not a bitter green—and it should not taste bitter. If it does, try a different kind or source.

How the kale is cooked is also important. Some cooking methods work better than others (see pages 23–33 for ways to cook kale).

And it is true that late fall kales taste better. This is their season, really. After a frost, the sugars become more prominent. The common wisdom is that the starches turn to sugar to protect the kale plant from the frost. Breeder Frank Morton's theory is that kales don't have heat or insects to contend with after a frost, and therefore their energy goes into producing a tastier leaf.

So, relax, learn the basic varieties, but don't fret.

Curly Kales or Scotch Kales

Varieties include: Winterbor, Starbor, Ripbor, Redbor, Dwarf Blue Curled Scotch and Beedy's Camden

The common kale we have come to know in the marketplace: a rich blue-green solid color with wavy, sometimes frilly, leaves. This kale can look the most formidable with large curly leaves, but cooked properly, it turns tender and pleasant. Good mild flavor, for every use: kale chips, salads, sautés, soups and sides.

Russian and Siberian Kales

Varieties include: Red Russian, White Russian, Siberian

The Red Russian kales distinguish themselves with their contrasting colors: oaklike blue-green leaves that are large lobed and jagged looking with red and purple veins throughout. The White Russian has white veining. Red Russian is probably the most tender and most delicate of the kales, and can even wilt on the way home from a farmers' market. The mild-flavored leaves can sometimes be sautéed right in the pan (without precooking or blanching), and they cook down more in volume than does curly kale. The red-purple hues (and sweet flavor) become more pronounced after a frost, but then change to green when cooked. (The color comes from anthocyanin pigments, which are water soluble.) For all uses, including smoothies, salads, sautés, soups and sides.

Italian Heirloom Kales (Dinosaur Kale)
Varieties include: Lacinato, Tuscan, Toscano, Tuscan Black, Cavolo Nero

These leaves are long, blue/green/black and straplike with savoyed (wrinkled) leaves, thus the "dinosaur" nickname. These sturdy kales have an excellent, mild flavor that gets sweeter tasting with a frost. This variety also cooks down more when sautéed, and quickly melts down in soups and stews. For every use: chips, soups, sides and salads. For salads, can often be massaged and tenderized, but sometimes the leaves are too tough to be eaten raw, depending on growing conditions and the age of the plant.

Baby Kale
Varieties include: Red Russian and lacinato

Baby kale is young kale, harvested at three to four weeks old, with small leaves that are only two to three inches long. Baby kale might be the Red Russian variety or an Italian variety, the same varieties we buy in bunches, but picked earlier. Baby kale is fairly new to supermarkets and farmers' markets. Supermarkets generally sell baby kale in plastic boxes, prewashed and ready to go. Farmers are bagging the young greens as they would baby lettuces and arugula. Baby kale is perfect for kale salads—no need to massage the leaves to tenderize them— they are already tender and flavorful. Baby kale can also be used in smoothies, quick sautés, soups and stews. (See page 33 for more about baby kale.)

Flower Sprouts
Varieties include: Kaleidoscope Mix

Flower sprouts is a new vegetable bred by crossing Brussels sprouts and kale. Think of mini bunches of kale— resembling more of a flower rosette or mini head of lettuce. This new variety was developed in England, and is now sold in the United States by Johnny's Selected Seeds. The Kaleidoscope variety offered by Johnny's is colorful mixture—green, purple and bicolor. "The tender mildly flavored sprouts have a taste and texture similar to Red Russian kale," the Johnny's catalog description reads. "Flower sprouts are suitable to diverse cooking methods such as lightly steaming, sautéing, stir-frying and roasting." The sprouts hold their color when cooked.

KALE: A NUTRITIONAL SUPERSTAR

Kale has been called a superstar, and even touted as such by superstars themselves. Whether it holds on to this status remains to be seen. But its superfood status is one aspect that won't change.

Kale is at the pinnacle when it comes to vegetables and nutrient content, according to health advocates.

The Center for Science in the Public Interest (CSPI) places kale as the number one healthiest vegetable, after rating and ranking 83 vegetables. Using a point system based on the overall percentages of vitamins, minerals, phytochemicals and fiber, kale easily secured the top spot with 1,381 points, surpassing all other vegetables the CSPI looked at. Broccoli, another vegetable touted for health, scored 263 points. Other top vegetables included sweet potatoes (485 points), spinach (672), red peppers (340), tomatoes (214) and Brussels sprouts (243).

While the nutritional advocacy group points to the benefits of all vegetables, it placed kale and 30 other top-scoring vegetables on a superstar list. If given a choice of vegetables in a situation, the CSPI recommended eating more of the superstar vegetables, such as kale, because their nutritional profiles "tower" over others'.

The reason to eat more vegetables overall is compelling, according to the center: Vegetable eaters had fewer strokes and a lower risk for heart attacks, to start. According to CSPI, people who averaged five or six servings of vegetables per day had an 18 percent lower risk of heart disease than did those who ate only one or two servings per day.

Kale also outshines both fruits and vegetables in the Aggregate Nutrient Density Index, now used by Whole Foods Market. The chain adopted this rating system in 2010 to help its customers pick the healthiest plant-based foods in its stores. Called ANDI for short, the system, developed by Dr. Joel Fuhrman, ranks plant-based foods from packaged to produce from zero to 1,000. Here, too, kale ranked number one, with a score of 1,000. (Collard greens also scored 1,000.) Next in line was bok choy, with a nutrient level score of 824. In comparison, strawberries received the highest ranking for fruit, with 212; blueberries, 130; flaxseeds, 85; apple juice, 16; and vanilla ice cream, 9.

Even outside of vegetables, kale is nearly always on the lists of the top 10 or 20 healthiest foods to eat. Those lists typically also include yogurt, wild salmon and beans, among other foods.

"I'm not a fan of the 'superfood' concept, but kale deserves to be among the foods regularly included in a healthy diet," says Walter Willett, chair of the department of nutrition at Harvard School of Public Health. "We find that about half of Americans have almost no dark leafy vegetables in their diet; it is usually spinach or nothing. Kale is a great source of many nutrients and important phytochemicals."

Here's a closer look at the nutrients of kale.

Top Kale

Kale contains so many nutrients, it's like a vitamin pill in itself. It's high in vitamins A, C and K, along with thiamine, riboflavin, niacin, vitamin B$_6$, folate and pantothenic acid. The minerals in kale include calcium, iron, potassium, magnesium, phosphorus, manganese, selenium, copper and zinc. Kale also contains protein, fiber and fatty acids, along with a series of phytonutrients.

Like Flaxseeds, Kale Offers Omega Fatty Acids

Salmon, flaxseeds and walnuts are a few of the foods typically suggested as sources for the essential fatty acids our body needs to stay healthy. Another source for these nutrients is leafy greens, especially kale. One serving of kale provides 121 mg of omega-3 fatty acids and 92.4 mg of omega-6. Omega fatty acids are especially important for controlling blood clotting and critical for healthy brain cells, among other health benefits. "New studies are identifying potential benefits [of omega-3 fatty acids] for a wide range of conditions including cancer, inflammatory bowel disease, and other autoimmune diseases such as lupus and rheumatoid arthritis," according to Dr. Frank Sacks, professor of cardiovascular disease prevention at Harvard University's School of Nutrition, an expert in this field. "Unfortunately, most Americans do not get enough of either type," says Sacks. "For good health, you should aim to get at least one rich source of omega-3 fatty acids in your diet every day."

Kale's Lutein and Zeaxanthin Aid Eye Health

"Kale is a great source of many nutrients and important phytochemicals, including carotenoids that play an important role in vision," says nutrition researcher Walter Willett. Two of those carotenoids, lutein and zeaxanthin, are cited as helping to reduce the risks of macular degeneration and cataracts, two common causes of vision loss as people age. In one Harvard health study, people with a history of eating lutein-rich foods, such as kale, had up to 22 percent lower risk for cataracts.

Kale and Healthy Bones

Kale is rich in both calcium and vitamin K. Its calcium content is higher than that of other calcium-strong vegetables, including spinach, arugula and broccoli. Per cup, kale contains 90 to 100 mg of calcium, more calcium per gram than whole milk. But researchers now point to vitamin K as key to bone health. In just ½ cup, kale contains 530 micrograms, or 684 percent, of the daily requirement of vitamin K, the highest amount of all the leafy greens. Several studies show that greater intake of vitamin K from leafy greens correlates with greater bone density in the spine, hips and other areas, and fewer fractures. A Tufts University study found that people who ate more than 250 micrograms of vitamin K daily had a 65 percent lower risk of hip fractures than did those who averaged 55 micrograms a day.

Kale's Potassium Power

Kale is an excellent source of potassium, with 299 micrograms in one cup, enough to provide 9 percent of the daily requirement for this mineral. One banana, another cited source for potassium, provides about 12 percent of the daily need. Potassium helps lower blood pressure and the risk of stroke. It may also boost bone density. Potassium acts as a natural diuretic to lower blood pressure and combat bloat. This, in turn, leads to proper kidney function, reduction in blood clotting and efficient opening of blood vessels. Potassium has also been shown to preserve muscle mass, in addition to helping nerves and muscles function properly. A deficiency in potassium can cause fatigue, irritability and increased blood pressure.

Kale for Beautiful Skin

Kale, and leafy greens in general, is touted for its impact on keeping skin smooth and younger looking. Vitamin A, an antiaging nutrient, can help prevent lines, wrinkles and dull skin. Kale is super rich in vitamin A, with 10,302 IU or 206 percent of daily requirements. With good levels of antioxidants—vitamin A, along with vitamin C—the skin is better able to fight oxidative stress from free radicals. Vitamin C (kale contains 134 percent of daily requirements) plays a role in building skin collagen, which keeps skin firm. Like meat, kale also contains all nine essential amino acids, plus nine other nonessential ones. In terms of skin health, amino acids help speed the repair and regeneration of skin cells and collagen.

Kale: An Anti-inflammatory

Anti-inflammatory foods have been in the news lately. Many believe that inflammation-causing foods, including sugar, trans fats and red and processed meats, are linked to increased risk of some diseases. Anti-inflammatory foods, on the other hand, can help counteract chronic inflammation, which can lead to heart disease; Alzheimer's; autoimmune diseases, such as rheumatoid arthritis; and certain cancers. Kale is considered a "strongly anti-inflammatory" food. Other foods to eat to maintain an anti-inflammatory "diet" include avocados; garlic; certain spices, such as turmeric; wild salmon; kelp; and extra-virgin olive oil.

Kale and Other Leafy Greens

Kale is a just one of many enjoyable leafy greens on the market. Many studies show the positive impact of eating leafy greens, of which kale towers.

According to the Center for Science in the Public Interest, these studies point to the benefits of eating more leafy greens:

- Women who consume more greens had less cognitive decline and memory loss than did those who ate few vegetables.
- Women who consumed the most leafy greens had about a 15 percent lower risk of diabetes.
- When men consumed about two servings of leafy greens a day, they had a 14 percent lower risk of colorectal cancer than did those who ate greens only once a week.
- In a study of men and women, the risk of stroke was about 20 percent lower for each serving of leafy greens that people ate.

Is Too Much Kale a Problem?

Kale took a beating in the news in December of 2013 when information came out about the effects cruciferous vegetables could have on the thyroid gland. Cruciferous vegetables, including kale, Brussels sprouts, broccoli, cauliflower and cabbages, are considered dietary goitrogens. Dietary goitrogens contain compounds called glucosinolates, which can interfere or compete with the way the thyroid picks up the iodine needed to produce the thyroid hormone. According to experts, it's not kale or another cruciferous vegetable on its own that increases the risk of an underactive thyroid or hypothyroidism (insufficient thyroid hormone), but a lack of adequate iodine levels.

Because of iodized salt, the majority of people in the country have adequate iodine levels, and therefore are not at risk for thyroid problems. For someone who is low in iodine, it is suggested that eating foods rich in iodine, such as seaweed, is a better way to address any potential problems, rather than giving up healthy cruciferous vegetables such as kale. In addition, cooking cruciferous vegetables dramatically lessens their goitrogenic properties.

"Basically the goitrogens are challenges to the thyroid. But in the absence of iodine deficiency, substantial or prolonged ingestion of dietary goitrogens and lastly the absence of an underlying thyroid disorder, the risk in this country of having problems in this area are very, very low, almost minuscule," according to Dr. Jeffrey Garber, chief of endocrinology at Harvard Vanguard Medical Associates and author of the latest clinical guidelines on hypothyroidism in adults. "Again, that's because the vast majority of people have adequate iodine levels to counteract the effect of goitrogens."

Shopping for Kale

Kale is available year-round, but its best seasons are the fall and spring. It is considered a fall-weather crop. In the fall, something magical happens to the plant—it gets sweeter in colder weather. When you go to farmers' markets in the spring, at least on the East Coast, you'll often find younger bunches of kale with smaller leaves. These are usually very tender and flavorful.

When shopping for kale in general, it's best to remember this fact: Not all kale is created equal.

Depending on where, when and how it's grown, kale can vary in both taste and texture. That might be good news, or occasionally, bad news.

Most of the time kale is tender when cooked, sweet and flavorful; or mildly chewy and pleasant when massaged for all kinds of salads. But I've also purchased kale that is too tough to cook through or massage—too chewy in the end and inedible. I've bought kale that has an unpleasant flavor after it's been cooked.

My best advice after years of preparing and writing about kale: Shop around.

Sample different varieties; but most important, sample different markets, farms and farmers' markets. The same variety might taste different depending on growing conditions, among other factors.

Look for growers that specialize in raising greens and try their kale. There are several of these here on Martha's Vineyard and I tend to gravitate toward their kale. Growers that specialize in greens often experiment with varieties and methods. They usually understand what kale plants need, such as the right soil preparation and the correct amount of water. Kale, as one farmer told me, does not tolerate stress very well. Summer heat and lack of water are two conditions that can affect the taste and tenderness of the leaf.

Supermarket kales can be fairly uniform, as grocery chains tend to use the same big suppliers. If you find some varieties you enjoy and that work well in your favorite recipes, you know you can count on this when you shop. I've had good luck at my local supermarket, as well at Whole Foods Market. For now, I know I can consistently use the curly kale from both places for raw salads—it tenderizes nicely when massaged, and the flavors are there when cooked. However, this can always change.

Even refrigeration can alter the taste of kale. "They're going to dry out the longer they are refrigerated," notes Lisa Fisher of Stannard Farms in Massachusetts. "They're not going to be as succulent." The freshness is a good reason to try farmers' markets or even your own backyard.

If you are lucky enough to have space in your yard for a garden, you can step out into the garden minutes before you about to cook kale or make a salad and pick just what you need. The plants in your home garden are always growing new leaves, so you are also getting younger, more tender kale.

Examine the Leaves

Every once in a while, you might find aphids congregating on the underside of kale leaves.

As unappealing as this is, I mention it as something to be aware of. Aphids are very tiny bugs, and if you're not looking, they can be hard to see. I suggest that you look carefully at the underside of a leaf or two.

Only occasionally have I found aphids. I usually

avoid buying kale from the supplier until the problem is cleared up. Aphids are not a common problem, but when they make an appearance, you'll at least notice them.

Storage

Moisture is the enemy of greens in cold storage. For this reason, I usually put a paper towel in the bag with the greens to help absorb excess moisture. There's no need to tie the bag up—often it's difficult to fit a bunch of kale into one bag anyway. If you rinse kale ahead of time, make sure you dry it well in a salad spinner before storing.

Another tip for easy storage and use: Remove the leaves from the stalks right away when you get the kale home. It takes only a few seconds to strip the leaves from the stalks, and it then becomes much easier to find the room to store it.

Stripping the Leaves from the Stalks

The best trick for removing the kale leaf from the stalk is to strip it off. Use one hand to hold the stalk of an individual leaf, rib side up. Use the other hand to strip the leaf off the stalk with one quick motion. Once you get this, a whole bunch can be stripped in seconds. Discard or compost the stalks. If stalks are tender, you can chop them up and use them. For juicing, use the whole leaf with its stalk intact. As one farmer told me, the stalks can be sweet even though they're a little tough to chew.

Washing and Drying Kale

Fill a large bowl with cool or cold water, add the greens, sluice them around, then lift them out of the water and place in a colander.

A salad spinner is a terrific time-saver in preparing kale. It dries the leaves better than towels or paper towels or a colander. It's especially helpful for the kale to be dry for salads, massaging and kale chips.

When I get a bunch of kale from the fridge or garden, I automatically reach for the salad spinner. You can fill it up with water, lift the greens out in the strainer and spin dry—all with one tool. I prefer the pull-cord spinners to the hand-cranked or push-button varieties because they seem to remove more water from the greens.

When you sauté or stir-fry kale, however, a little moisture on a leaf doesn't matter as much, and sometimes can be helpful in keeping the kale from sticking to the pan.

If your tender kale gets limp like lettuce, fill the salad spinner with very cold water and soak the kale for 10 to 15 minutes. It perks right up.

Ways to Cook Kale

As you try recipes in the book, you will learn all the different ways to cook kale. I can't recall another vegetable that is so versatile in the ways it can be prepared and enjoyed.

In the recipes that follow, kale is sautéed, precooked or boiled, simmered or braised, baked, grilled, stir-fried, massaged or enjoyed raw in a salad or smoothie.

My goal in writing this cookbook is for people to become comfortable with handling and cooking kale. I suggest trying a variety of these cooking techniques in the beginning. You'll see the differences and eventually intuitively know the right method for the outcome you are seeking.

Most of the kale varieties you find in markets are interchangeable. So you can use these methods I describe here with most all of the kale you purchase or grow.

Volume reduction during cooking is one important difference between the curly kale versus the Red Russian and Italian kales. The curly kale will generally hold more of its volume—in other words, it won't shrink down as much as the Red Russian or Italian varieties.

This might be useful in determining how much to use for serving portions, as well as what you'll need for a certain dish. When I use kale as a bed for fish, for example, much as spinach is often used, I like to use the Italian or Red Russian varieties. These cook down more, and neatly fit under a piece of fish that should be the star in the instance. When I want a side dish for more people, I generally pick the curly kale that precooks beautifully and holds its shape and volume. I usually pick curly kale for kale chips as well, for the same reason.

GREENS: THE WHOLE PICTURE

Let's step back for a minute and put kale into perspective, looking at the whole world of leafy greens. The grouping of greens by family is a helpful indication of the best ways to cook a particular type.

The succulent Asian greens in the Cruciferae family—napa cabbage, Chinese cabbage and bok choy—are considered dark leafy greens, even if light in color. They are mild-flavored, often delicate, and their stalks, stems and leaves have a high water content. Because of the water content, when a leaf or stalk hits a hot pan, it becomes tender and juicy quickly. Overcooking is generally the problem with Asian greens, which taste best crisp-tender.

It makes sense that Asian flavorings are typically used on Asian greens, but stir-frying or even quick sautéing is ideal for this family of greens.

The next family grouping is the *Chenapodium* greens—spinach, beet greens and Swiss chard. These greens are mild-tasting and tender as well, easily cooked by wilting in a hot skillet. A few tablespoons of water might be all that's needed to keep them from sticking. Sauté this type of green with onions and garlic, directly in the pan, with a cover if needed, to hold in heat and moisture.

The more bitter greens—mustard, turnip and dandelion greens, broccoli rabe—often need special treatment. Certain foods are known to complement the flavor and reduce the bitterness; these include olive oil, garlic, pork fat, eggs, vinegar, lemon juice, cheese, tomatoes or bread. These greens can benefit from either a quick hot sauté with accompaniments that tame the bitterness. Or you can temper the bitterness a bit by a quick precooking in water; here, a bit of the bitterness leaches into the water and leaves a more palatable green.

Finally, we come to kale and collard greens, which are similar in many ways. Both are in the Cruciferae family, with large leafy leaves, often somewhat thick. Although some characterize these as bitter greens, they are not. Unless grown incorrectly and stressed by heat, insects or insufficient watering, kale and collards generally are sweet- or pleasant-tasting.

The emphasis here is on cooking the leaves so they are tender and easy to chew, and on flavorings. Neither kale or collards really taste good on their own without at least some accompaniment, whether it's garlic and olive oil, caramelized onion, a bit of sweetness from a raisin or piece of fruit or richness from an avocado or a shaving of cheese.

One of the biggest surprises when it comes to cooking kale and collards, and the bitter greens as well, is how lousy they can look and taste after being steamed.

This seems counterintuitive. But in my tests over the years, steaming greens resulted in grayish or army green vegetables—not very attractive—and often tasting stronger and/or more bitter.

The reason is that leafy greens contain their own acids that, when heated, come into contact with the plant's chlorophyll and turn it gray. In essence, the acid in the plant itself destroys its own color. You can dramatize this effect by adding lemon, tomato or vinegar to greens as they cook: The bright green chlorophyll quickly turns an unappealing army green. You can see happen when cooking kale in a soup with tomatoes, too. When you steam greens, the same thing happens.

If you cook greens in a large pot of water, however, the acids are diluted and the vegetables tend to stay bright green. It also affects the flavor of bitter greens by diluting the bitterness and mellowing the flavor. This is the effect or parboiling or precooking kale, used in a number of recipes in this book—though with far less water than a large pot.

The same effect will happen, happily, in a small amount of water, such as 2 to 4 cups. As long as there is some water left in the pot after cooking the kale, this method works its magic. Parboiling works well for softening large, tough kale leaves, and is fast as well, requiring only four to five minutes to completely cook the leaves. To me, it's preferable to ten to fifteen minutes of sautéing, even with liquid added.

With this method, you can drink the kale cooking water like tea. This "potlikker" as it is sometimes called, can be a tasty broth that captures nutrients otherwise lost in the cooking.

KALE COOKING METHODS AT A GLANCE
Precooking or Shallow Blanching

This is my own preferred method for cooking kale for many side dishes. A good starter recipe is the Kale with Raisins and Pine Nuts (page 154). Over the years, I've found this is one of the best recipes for introducing beginners to cooked kale.

Use the widest sauté pan you have, with a lid, so the greens can spread out and cook quickly. A wide-based soup pot works too. Bring about 4 cups of water to a boil and plunge in the greens—a whole bunch that has been stemmed and cut into bite-size pieces. Boil for four to six minutes, depending on the type and age. A tender Italian kale or Red Russian can take just a few minutes. Test a leaf, and when it tastes tender and good, it's done. Drain in a colander, and shake a number of times to release the steam and stop the cooking. You can cook greens ahead this way as well.

I then take the cooked greens and add them to a sauté—cooked onion, garlic, leeks, shallots, ginger sautéed in oil– something that gives them a nice flavor. Add a few pinches of salt. At the end, you can squirt in a little lemon or lime juice.

Although it does take two steps, I find in the end, it's faster that sautéing the greens directly in the pan from the start.

If you are cooking a pasta or grain in a big pot of water, add the kale during the last few minutes, then drain the mixture and add your sauce. This method works great with curly kales that can be slightly tougher than Red Russian or Italian varieties.

Sautéing

Kale can be sautéed directly in a skillet, with some flavorings. Typically, you start with a tablespoon or so of olive oil, and a bit of garlic, ginger, onions, leeks or shallots. After the chosen aromatic is cooked, add your washed and chopped kale. This is a good time to have a bit of the water still clinging to the leaves after rinsing. (It's easiest to cut greens first, then rinse.) Sauté the greens, stirring for a few minutes until reduced in volume, then cover, lower the heat and continue to cook until tender. Although the greens may look cooked after wilting, they typically need a bit more time to cook thoroughly enough that they are not unpleasantly chewy. Check once or twice during the cooking to make sure the kale isn't sticking. If it is, add a tablespoon or two of water or stock. This method works better with very tender kale, such as the Italian or Red Russian kales, as well as baby kale.

Stir-frying

Stir-frying is quick cooking, with a higher heat and constant movement, and can work well with kale. Cut the kale into bite-size pieces or thin strips, then add the oil and the greens at the same time, using tongs to constantly move the kale around. As the moving pieces hit the high heat, the greens cook quickly.

Sometimes, when the recipe warrants it, you can combine the kale with an Asian green, such as napa cabbage, or another vegetable. The liquid released from the juicier vegetable helps create a bit of liquid and keeps the greens from sticking. In the Fried Rice with Greens (page 102), the kale cooks with napa cabbage, and then carrots, corn, ginger and garlic are added. All the vegetables cook together in five to six minutes before the sauce is added.

If the kale is stir-fried on its own for a side dish, it's best to add such aromatics as garlic, ginger or scallions a minute or two into the cooking, so they don't burn in the hot pan.

Braising

Using liquid to cook kale softens the greens, and depending on the liquid, can flavor kale and the whole dish. The main difference between precooking or blanching kale is that the aromatics are added to the pan first, then the kale, then a liquid. My Braised Kale and Chicken dish (page 205) is a good example. After the onion is sautéed, the kale and vegetables are sautéed briefly before adding the chicken stock, apple cider and chicken. The cover goes on and everything is cooked in the hot, flavored liquid, which creates a sauce within the dish.

When the aromatics are cooked first before a braising liquid is added, they form the flavor foundation of a braised dish. Typically, meat or chicken is browned first in a pan. The added liquid—wine, water, stock or a combination—picks up the browned bits and then cooks the meat or chicken and vegetables.

The braising can be even simpler when it comes to kale. You can sauté a few aromatics, add the kale and some liquid, cover, and cook. It can be as little as half a cup of water or stock to a few cups.

Like other vegetables, kale can be braised in the oven.

Baking or Roasting

With the invention of kale chips, this method could already be the most popular way to cook kale. A whole kale bunch is reduced to light, crispy, salty pieces in the heat of the oven.

To roast kale to crispiness, wash a bunch of kale, strip from its stalks and dry in a salad spinner. Tear the leaves into larger-than-bite-size pieces (they'll shrink during baking). Drizzle with enough oil to coat the leaves, and work the oil into the nooks and crevices with your fingers. Sprinkle with salt. Line one or two baking pans with parchment for easy cleanup. About 4 cups of kale, maybe half a bunch, fits on a standard baking sheeting without too much initial crowding. Set the temperature at 300°F and roast until crispy, not burned, about 20 minutes. You can experiment with temperatures from 275° to 375°F, and see what works best in your oven.

But roasting kale is not confined to kale chips. Try the homemade granola (page 50), where kale and oats are baked together. It's a great snack or breakfast.

There is also the stage between raw and crispy, where kale softens and cooks and makes a great side dish— before it becomes crispy.

This is a good method to use with a bag of different kales, maybe different shades of pinks, greens and purple, sometimes bagged together at farmers' markets. Rub with oil, sprinkle with salt, place on a sheet pan and bake at 325° or 350°F. Mix a few times, and taste occasionally as you turn it over with tongs. Remove when it tastes good but before it's crispy, 12 to 15 minutes, though a few edges will get crispy here and there, which is nice. Add a sprinkling of cheese or a drop or two of citrus juice.

Try roasting kale with another vegetable or multiple vegetables, such as potatoes, cauliflower, carrots, parsnips, turnips or beets. The denser vegetables usually take longer, so start those first, then add torn pieces of kale rubbed with oil. Served on a platter, the supporting vegetables look and taste great together. Try the Roasted Cauliflower and Kale (page 152), using either olive oil or browned butter.

FLAVORS AND FOODS KALE LOVES

These are some of the foods that go particularly well with kale—that flavor or complement it. All foods have their affinities—often you instinctively know what foods work well together. Whole food cultures revolve around pairing foods, and this can help in creating dishes.

Kale is a particularly friendly vegetable. It has many friends and partners. In fact, it prefers to be in the company of others, rather than by itself.

Cooking with Kale

Aromatics

Garlic	Ginger	Leeks	Onions, red or yellow	Shallots

Salty and/or Meaty

Bacon	Chicken stock	Chorizo, smoked sausage	Mushrooms, all types	Olives	Pancetta, prosciutto
Parmigiano-Romano, feta, blue cheese	Salami	Salt! (kosher or sea)	Soy sauce		

Spices and Herbs

Basil	Bay leaf	Black pepper	Cayenne pepper	Chili flakes	Chili powder
Cilantro	Coriander	Cumin	Curry	Garam masala	Mint
Oregano	Rosemary	Sweet smoked paprika	Thyme		

Sweet

Dried fruit: raisins, cranberries, currants, cherries	Honey	Maple syrup

Acidic—Juice and zest of:

Lemon	Lime	Orange

Dairy

Blue cheese	Butter	Cheddar cheese	Feta (especially Greek or French sheep's milk)	Goat cheese
Gruyère cheese, Swiss cheese	Heavy cream, crème fraîche	Ricotta salata	Sour cream	Yogurt

Foods to Pair with Kale

White Foods

Cauliflower	Eggs	Flounder, fluke, sole, cod, halibut	Pasta (regular and whole wheat)	Potatoes
Rice (and whole grains, such as quinoa and farro)		Tofu	White beans (and other beans)	

Meats, Chicken, Fish

Chicken, roasted or grilled	Clams	Mussels	Pork	Salmon	Shrimp
Steak, grilled	Tuna	White fish: sole, flounder, halibut			

Vegetables

Beets	Bell peppers, red or yellow	Broccoli	Brussels sprouts	Cabbages	Carrots
Cauliflower	Corn	Mushrooms	Parsnips	Potatoes	Rutabaga
Squash	Sweet Potatoes	Tomatoes			

Best Kale Salad Components

Fruits

Apple	Apricot	Blackberries	Blueberries	Coconut	Dates
Dried cherries	Dried cranberries	Figs	Grapefruit	Lemon	Lime
Mango	Orange	Peach	Pear	Pineapple	Plum
Pomegranate	Raspberries	Strawberries	Watermelon		

Vegetables

Avocado	Cabbage	Carrot	Celery	Corn	Cucumber
Endive	Fennel	Frisée	Onion, red	Pepper, red or yellow	Radishes
Tomato					

Nuts and Seeds

All kinds of tree nuts, especially walnuts, pine nuts, almonds, hazelnuts, pecans	Peanuts	Pumpkin seeds	Sesame seeds	Sunflower seeds

Dressings

Balsamic, sherry, or other vinegar	Lemon juice	Lime juice	Olive oil	Orange juice	Peanut oil, sesame oil

Fresh Herbs

Basil	Chives	Mint	Oregano	Parsley	Rosemary
Thyme					

Grilling

Grilling kale comes in handy sometimes, especially in the summer when you are grilling other foods. Spread out, the kale leaf cooks quickly under medium heat, and can burn if you don't keep an eye on it. The speediness here makes it easy to cook kale in between, before, or after whatever else you are grilling.

The Grilled Kale and Tomato Panzanella Salad (page 140) is a wonderful recipe and good starting place to try this method. A homemade dressing added to warm, grilled kale greens is delicious.

Unless you are using a perforated grill pan, it's easier to keep the kale leaf attached to its stem while it's grilled. Rub about a tablespoon of oil into a bunch of washed and dried kale. With your hands, work the oil into the leaves, as in the early stages of massaging kale. Sprinkle with salt and lay the leaf spread out on a grill—you can almost fit a whole bunch on a standard gas grill. Grill for about 2 minutes per side, on medium or medium-low heat. The edges start to get crispy, maybe browned a tiny bit, but most of the leaf remains soft. A bit of the smokiness we associate with grilling flavors the kale as well. Cut the leaf from the rib with scissors or a knife.

This method works indoors, too, with a grill pan or stovetop grill that covers two burners.

MASSAGING KALE

Eyebrows get raised when "massaging kale" comes up. It leads to comments—even cartoons.

My Canadian friend and fellow cookbook author Charmian Christie says if she had a choice, she would come back in the next life as kale.

©Rick Galat

"Carrots get stripped and shredded to pieces. Potatoes have their eyes gouged out before being mashed to a pulp, and we won't discuss what happens to poor old butternut squash. But kale? I kid you not, it gets slathered in oil and given a rubdown," says Charmian, author of *The Messy Baker: More than 75 Delicious Recipes from a Real Kitchen.* "Yeah. I'd definitely come back as kale."

This technique needs a new name, a friend suggested. We came up with "kneading" kale. But it could be too late, since those who massage kale already know what it means, and writing "kneading" in a recipe could cause confusion.

What is massaging, what is the basic technique and which kale varieties benefit most?

Massaging kale for raw kale salads came into vogue as the raw food movement blossomed in the past decade. When I wrote a book on leafy greens in 1996—no one ate raw kale. And it's not surprising. An uncooked kale leaf is fibrous and tough, too chewy to enjoy. Anyone who has munched on a raw piece of kale knows this.

Massaging it, though, makes uncooked kale edible, even enjoyable. As you work on the kale leaf, gently rubbing oil and salt into the curls and valleys, you can see visible changes. It reduces in size, softens and becomes almost silky. The kale leaf darkens and appears cooked. At this point, you can use it in a salad on its own with a vinaigrette, or paired with a grain or pasta.

"When you massage kale, you break down the fibers and make it easier to digest," explains Deneen McQueen-Chippari, a nutrition coach and owner of Whole Soul Wellness based in Hingham, Massachusetts.

Massaged kale makes a great base. The green color is vibrant and the kale pairs beautifully with many fruits, vegetables, dried fruits and nuts. Massaged kale can also be used in dishes from meat loaf to veggie burgers to potato kale latkes.

Depending on where you look, massaging techniques run the gamut: Some use olive oil, and rub it into the kale for several minutes. Others work salt into the greens. Still others employ citrus, such as lemon juice, or citrus juice and oil, and massage that mixture. Some even massage the kale with the salad dressing and let it sit. After trial and error, I've had the most luck with using oil and salt together. The salt adds friction but also gets carried by the oil, which helps you coat each part of the leaf more easily. And that's where the massaging or kneading comes in. You use both hands getting right into the bowl with your fingers and thumbs to coat and "rub down" the pieces. Two or three minutes usually does the trick, getting to each and every leaf, sometimes more than once. Keep in mind your pile of kale will reduce by about half, depending on the variety of the kale. You know you are done massaging when the kale starts to taste good.

Massaging Kale: A Basic Recipe

4–6 cups kale (1 typical bunch), any variety

2–3 teaspoons olive oil

¼ teaspoon kosher salt (about 2 good pinches), or extra as needed

1. First, strip the kale from the stalk. Chop or tear the kale leaves into ribbons or bite-size pieces, depending on how you want it to look.

2. Rinse the kale and make sure it's as dry as possible. A salad spinner works perfectly for cleaning kale and other greens.

3. Place the kale into a large bowl—large enough to get your hands into, to toss the kale. Add the olive oil—2 teaspoons for about 4 cups, or 1 tablespoon for 4 or more cups. Add the kosher salt—2 pinches for 4 cups, ½ teaspoon for more than 4 cups.

4. Massage or rub the pieces for 2 to 3 minutes, trying to coat each and every leaf.

Types of Kale to Massage

Massaging isn't foolproof, however. Some kale is so tough it won't soften, like beans that just won't cook. Like me, you've probably encountered the occasional kale salad that's just too chewy to enjoy.

I had this happen when testing a kale Caesar salad for the book. I used a dressing I knew was delicious, and a recipe I had made before with success. I massaged and massaged a head of lacinato kale, but the kale stayed tough and chewy. We tried a couple of bites, but that was all we could manage. We let the kale salad sit overnight in the dressing, still no difference.

This generally has more to do with how the kale was grown than with any massaging technique. If you have kale too tough to massage, try another variety or buy from a different source.

All types of mature kale seem to work. I tend to gravitate toward the curly or the lacinato (dinosaur) kale; they soften but also hold up. The Red Russian kale, one of the most tender of all the kales, can look a bit limp in a salad, though for use in loaves or pasta dishes, it works very well.

Vary the Massaged Flavors

Try different oils for aroma, depending on the recipe. Dark sesame oil adds a distinctive flavor for an Asian dish. For a noodle salad with a spicy peanut sauce, I'll use peanut oil if I have it. Coconut oil adds a luscious flavor. You can then top the salad with avocado or other vegetables or fruit, such blueberries or dried apricots and maybe a sprinkling of shredded coconut.

Try different salts or a flavored salt with rosemary or smoked salt.

Add the juice of a fresh orange or lemon. Alternatively, the zest from a nonsprayed lemon, lime or orange can be added after an initial massage with olive oil and salt.

Add the dressing of your choice once the kale is massaged. Here, the sky is the limit to varying your salads, from mustard to maple and garlic to ginger. Kale is like chicken or tofu in that it takes on the flavors of what's being added.

Other Uses for Massaged Kale

Now that young, tender baby kale with leaves two to three inches in length is readily available, you have a choice for salads. Should you feature baby kale or massaged kale? What works best where? Sometimes it will be based on what you have available in your garden, fridge or market.

Baby kale is what I choose first for salads that will feature mainly the greens themselves. Straight kale salad, say, with avocados and Parmesan cheese or a few ripe tomatoes and cucumbers in the summer, is easier to eat and enjoy when the kale is young and tender.

But for massaged kale, there are plenty of other uses:

Make a grain salad: Chopped and massaged kale forms a great partner with many grains, holding its own with quinoa, farro, cracked wheat and almost any other type of grain salad you can think of. Add a few vegetables and a simple citrus dressing, and your friends will rave. Chop it into bite-size or smaller bits and massage. Once dressed, massaged kale and grain salads taste good the next day because the kale doesn't wilt like dressed lettuce.

Beans and kale form a nutritional powerhouse that also tastes good. The kale breaks up the beans' texture. Try black beans and kale with radishes and a fruit salsa dressing. The chickpea-kale combo with kalamata olives, roasted red pepper and feta fits perfectly on a buffet table or with grilled mains.

Make pasta dishes, especially pasta salads: Try the Asian Peanut Noodle and Kale Salad (page 115).

There are multiple approaches you can use with roasted or poached chicken and massaged kale.

Use in beef, turkey or veggie burgers and meat or turkey loaves. In the past I've added spinach or Swiss chard to lasagna; now, I usually substitute massaged kale—it finishes cooking in the dish. Veggie Burgers with Kale (page 105) are better looking than most veggie burgers, and easier, too. I've even added massaged kale bits to latkes—and love the contrasting color and flavor.

If you chop the kale into small bits before massaging it, you can use it as a substitute for parsley, especially for its color and nutrition (though parsley is also full of nutrients). If it's too challenging to massage as bits, you can cut it into bite-size pieces, massage it and then chop it a bit more.

Growing Kale

How kale is grown can give great insight into the flavor and taste of kale. In fact, it is probably more important than the variety of kale itself.

Tips from kale experts not only can help you grow better kale in your backyard garden, but also assist in finding the best-tasting kale. Certain growing practices can make one kale taste better than another kale. Certainly, the seasons make a difference, too.

Most vegetables have a distinct season, such as summer for tomatoes and corn, fall for squashes, and spring for asparagus and certain greens. Kale really has two seasons: spring and fall; it grows better in colder weather than in very hot weather.

Frank Morton, for example, an expert in growing and breeding kale, says he maintains two growing seasons for kale. He starts in January the plants that he grows in the spring, and then seeds again in July, for plants he grows in the fall.

"You should eat your vegetables in the right time of the year," he notes.

"I don't eat leeks in the summer and I don't eat kale in the summer." Morton explains, "Some of my friends grow kale all summer long; I don't. What often happens to kale in summer, it gets stressed; it gets aphids. If it's grown in hot weather, it's going to taste bitter and hot. It tastes like kale grown in the summer."

If you grow kale, you know it can persevere through the fall long after other plants are put to bed. It can grow after a snowstorm and even through the winter, in some cases. Seed catalogs capture it best, with such terms as "cold hearty" or "best surviving kale." You'll see growers talk about a type of kale, what temperatures it

can withstand and whether or not it overwinters. Some kale names are descriptive in this way, too: Long Seasons, Russian Hunger, Siberian. "It got to eleven degrees this winter; plants were fine and happy." It's surprising there wasn't a surge in interest in growing kale years ago.

Whereas we might wither in winter, cover up and hibernate, kale is among the few hardy plants left in a garden, maybe with the leeks and carrots. Not only does it survive when other plants cannot, it is actually improved by a frost—it becomes sweeter. Kale is hard-wired to protect itself in cold weather, specifically after a frost, when the starches in the plant turn to sugar.

But for many farmers, and most home growers, kale is started the spring and grown through the summer and the fall, sometimes into winter. Good growing conditions are important.

To Lisa Fisher, and other greens growers, it comes down to three elements: "Food, water and bugs."

Soil First

Fisher owns Stannard Farms on Martha's Vineyard, where she specializes in growing all sorts of greens from mizuna and arugula to collards and kale. She stresses the use of well-balanced compost. She has chickens and composts their manure, great for nitrogen, which greens devour.

She digs trenches for rows of greens and puts the compost in the bottom of each trench, four to six inches down, and rakes soil over the compost before planting. "Rather than put it all over the garden, I concentrate on the row I'm planting."

"You have to have a nice fertile soil," says Paul Gallione of Johnny's Selected Seeds and an organic grower himself. "This is one of the most important things with kale." The pH range should be in the 6 to 7 range, high in organic matter with good drainage.

Water

"Watering is a big part of it." says Fisher, who grows throughout the summer.

An important tool for her is a rain gauge, which tells her how much it rained in a particular week. Her rule of thumb is about an inch of water a week for greens. "That is really quite a lot," she says.

"I have a watering schedule I stick to." She runs her overhead sprinklers for three hours twice a week, usually between three and six a.m., including the morning before she picks for the farmers' market.

Paul from Johnny's agrees: Water is key.

"[Kale] will grow wonderfully through the summer, but you need to have sufficient, regular moisture, that's what is going to keep the flavor nice for you," he says. "If it grows through a dry spell, it's going to more tough and bitter. If it's not watered properly, the plants will be stressed."

Pests

Kale plants can be subject to aphids and cabbage worms. One method to prevent insects is the use of row covers, staked high enough for the plants to grow.

For cabbage worms (you'll first notice the white moths flying around the plants), try *Bacillus thuringiensis*, or Bt, a certified organic insecticide.

FRANK MORTON: THE KALE WHISPERER

When I called Frank Morton, at home on Gathering Together Farm in Philomath, Oregon, he was able talk on the subject of kale for more than two hours. A farmer and seed collector for 30 years, his pioneering work first in lettuces—growing up to 84 varieties—led others to call him a genius in the fields. When he turned his hyper attention to kale, it was the late '80s, long before it became a household fascination.

He's responsible for the White Russian kale now appearing in markets, a green leafy kale with white, silvery veins and a growing favorite among chefs. It's a cross between the Red Russian kale, the flatter-looking kale with spidery purple veins, and Siberian kale, a broad-leafed and hardy green kale.

The Rainbow lacinato seeds sold by Fedco, an organic seed company based in Maine, also come from Frank.

"Who but Frank Morton would think to cross lacinato with Redbor," the Fedco catalog says about Rainbow lacinato, "a stunning new kale that combines some of the best features of both. It looks like dinosaur kale overlaid with red, blues and purples."

"What has happened to kale is a remarkable thing for me to have watched," says Frank, who remembers his mother, when he was a youngster, being given so much garden kale she washed it in a washing machine. "I love that story." He doesn't remember liking kale as a kid, but says, "I've liked kale ever since I've become a farmer, 30 years ago.

"Back in the '80s no one was eating kale, I can tell you. I started to notice the change in the '90s. I think people started going crazy for kale in 2005 and 2007. It's verging on becoming irritating," he jokes. "I shouldn't say that; I sell a lot of kale."

His seed company, Wild Garden Seed (wildgardenseed.com) sells his specialized kale varieties, along with lettuces and other garden vegetables and flowers.

His theory is that it all started when somebody invented the kale chip. "People started coming up with all sorts of ideas for using it."

"I think part of this grew out of the salad world and the world of greens that started coming to people in those days—mizuna, arugula, radicchio, Asian mustards, I think that introduced people to the idea there's a world of greens out there."

Frank said his interest in plant breeding grew out of an accidental cross between one type of lettuce and another, and it opened his eyes to where new varieties came from. "I was struck one day by the potential of cross pollinating different varieties. It came out of me being a seed saver."

Using the cross between Red Russian and Siberian kale, he explains how it happens—and says it takes about eight generations of planting selected seeds side by side to get to where you might want to go.

Red Russian kale, he explains, has purple stems and green pointy leaves; Siberian kale, rounded green leaves with no red pigment.

When you plant a hybrid, you get what looks like an average between the parents.

But he says, when you grow a hybrid out, and get the

seeds, you see something far more interesting: the genetic spectrum. In the field of kale plants, there are bright green to bright red hues and new shapes, combined and distributed in different ways. Those traits can also be exaggerated in one way or another. For example, a plant might have extra-lacy leaves similar in shape to those of mizuna, or a plant may have just a little bit of leaf. "Way back then, I accidentally created the moss curled kale. I haven't released that."

In this wild garden kale mix, he says, essentially all the genetics were there that gave rise to new varieties he's credited with: Red Ursa, the White Russian and Red Ruffled, as well as "a whole bunch of other shapes and forms that never really got named. That all came from the cross of red Russian and Siberian," he says.

As a plant breeder, Frank is quick to differentiate himself from corporate plant breeders that deliberately set out to create a plant with specific traits, such as a certain plant wall thickness, using gene guns and microscopes. "You can do that, but you miss a lot of cool stuff along the way. Me and a lot of other people before me, just watch the process happen."

"You have to realize the word *gene* was not invented until 100 years ago.

"Our forebears created the crops we use today by exactly the same methods I've been using for past 30 years. It's mostly intuitive, mostly by observing.

"You don't need to do a darn thing; that's the great thing about nature."

To get the first cross between two varieties, Frank says he grows out two types of kale plants near each other, and lets bees cross-pollinate them.

"You need at least a dozen plants of each one. Some people say you need 60 in kale; I like to have 30 plants." Every plant, he says, is an individual, like people—different not only in the way they look but also with slightly different disease resistance genes or survival traits.

In the first generation, you get that average between two. He collects seeds from the plants he likes, and repeats this.

"In the second generation, you see the whole rainbow, all these possibilities. Each possibility, a plant breeder can turn into a family line."

He then walks. He walks through 300 plants and sees the one that he likes. He walks through another 300 plants and picks another. "By walking the whole field, I get those together and let them flower together." Along the way, he's protecting and furthering certain traits and weeding out others. "It's way more important what you throw out," he explains. "If you don't throw out the bad stuff, it will just keep coming around."

In subsequent generations, different variations pop up. "Over the next seven generations, you decide what it is you like, and grow those out one generation after another. I try to see what they want to become. It's like shuffling a deck of cards and dealing out new hands. He says it takes about eight generations to get to where he wants to go.

From this process came their award-winning new variety, Red Ursa, combining the broad frills of Siberian kale with the color of Red Russian. In the national gardening trials, Red Ursa was selected as one of the top five new vegetable introductions in 1997, described as very sweet, colorful and with a great raw flavor for salads.

From this same process and original varieties also came the White Russian variety, another with recognized flavor. That one can now be found in national supermarkets.

What does he look for in kale plants?

The first is color, he says. "That's the first thing everyone responds to—you're never going to taste it if you don't like the look of it."

He points out that when it comes to kale, color is equivalent to nutrition.

"All color in plants are antioxidants; that is not an overstatement. When you select for brightness of color, you are selecting for nutrition. It's not just eye candy, it's nutrition."

Flavor, of course, is important.

To develop the Rainbow lacinato, for example, Frank planted the lacinato kale, a kale with good flavor, together with a hybrid, Redbor, a stunning purple kale. "I wanted purple lacinato."

The Redbor variety doesn't have a lot of flavor, but some other great qualities—terrific cold hardiness, strong stems and disease resistance in addition to the bold color.

"My assumption was over time, we'd find plants that would have the good taste, because we're always tasting. But at first, you have to get a plant that will grow and will make it to market."

He started this process for Rainbow lacinato in 2003—a full 10 years ago, and it's still not exactly where he wants to be with this new plant after six generations, throwing out plants with problems and keeping what they like.

"Most of them are becoming what they want to be." At the end of this process, Frank says they may well have three or more different varieties, in addition to the rainbow kale.

The other very important piece of the puzzle is understanding the seasons and best growing conditions for kale, to avoiding such stressors as heat or insects that attack kale, which causes it to produce a chemical that changes the taste of the plant.

Kales seasons are spring and fall, colder rather than warmer growing conditions. The natural cycle for kale is July to July, he explains. "If you start kale in the spring, you're already not on the natural cycle. It's grown too long, gets too big." He plants in January for a spring crop, and then again in July, for a fall crop. He skips the summer altogether. "If you grow them in the manner in which they were intended and have evolved into, they have less stress, they taste better."

Frank says they also plant their kale plants closer together, spacing them about one foot apart, rather than the typical spacing of two feet. That keeps the plant from forming a few big leaves, and encourages a lot of smaller leaves. "We grow our kale plants to the state of young maturity, and we harvest the young mature leaves."

Frank speculates that had the market not changed in the direction of kale, he might not have sold all these kales.

"Lucky for me, I developed these things twenty years ago, and voilà, the world suddenly discovered kale and I suddenly realize I'm sitting on a gold mine."

And he suspects his mother would be proud of his work.

"Kale is such a terrific plant. My mother would be so happy if she were alive."

Ingredients and Techniques

INGREDIENTS

Salt

It seems that no matter what I'm cooking, I always put a good amount of focus on salt. Salt is a simple ingredient, and it also happens to be a controversial one. In cooking, I find it essential. Kale is no exception.

Salt is the prime coaxer that brings out or heightens the flavors of the various ingredients. Sometimes a kale dish or soup, for example, will taste bland even though it has a pile of ingredients—and all that's missing is a little additional salt to make it more flavorful.

So, my easiest bit of cooking advice is to add enough salt to bring out all the elements. For any dish, add it a bit at a time, tasting as you go. In this way, also you can often see (and understand) the simple transformation salt can make. Obviously you don't want anything to taste salty, but just before it's salty is generally the spot you want to stop adding salt.

After I've sautéed kale for any side dish, I add a few pinches of salt. I mix and then taste to see if that was enough salt, or whether another pinch is warranted.

What about the type of salt? Any type—sea salt, kosher salt or regular table salt will do the trick of flavoring.

All of the recipes in this book were made and tested with Diamond kosher salt, a salt with large crystals, free of additives. Because of the size and shape of the crystals in kosher salts, it has less sodium per teaspoon than do regular table salt, sea salt and even Morton's kosher salt. So, if you use regular table salt or sea salt, you should probably cut the amount of salt in half, to start, and taste test from there.

The differences in the sodium content of various salts make it difficult to specify accurate amounts of salt in a recipe. For this reason, I don't always give a specific amount. I figure that people can salt their own food, to the level they prefer.

Freshly Ground Black Pepper

Black pepper in the ingredients list always means freshly ground black pepper. Freshly ground black pepper has a vibrant taste with a spicy bite. Preground pepper quickly loses its flavorful oils. It's worthwhile to invest in a good pepper mill if you don't have one.

Extra-Virgin Olive Oil

When a recipe calls for olive oil, in all cases it means extra-virgin olive oil, unless another type of oil, such as canola or coconut, is specified. Extra-virgin olive oil is pressed directly from olives, processed without chemicals or heat. It's better for you, and imparts flavor to your kale dishes, whether hot or cold.

Feta Cheese

See the sidebar (page 100) on the different types of feta cheese.

Parmesan Cheese

When available and when you want characteristic Parmesan flavor, choose Parmigiano-Reggiano cheese—the authentic Parmesan from Italy. It is a balanced, flavorful and mildly salty cheese—a little goes a long way, which is good because it can also be expensive.

In the soup chapter, you will also find reference to Parmesan rinds. The rind from a wedge of Parmesan cheese, preferably Parmigiano-Reggiano, adds complexity and depth to a soup made with water instead of stock. Like a bay leaf, the rind flavors the soup and then is pulled out and discarded when the soup is finished. You can buy precut Parmesan rinds or save your own rind and freeze until needed.

Panko Bread Crumbs

Panko bread crumbs are Japanese-style bread crumbs that are lightly crispy and crunchy right out of the box. I use them, primarily because they are so convenient, for a topping or filler in a meat loaf. I will also typically add a few teaspoons of oil to the bread crumbs and a bit of salt or Parmesan cheese for quick flavor. Then I toss them on top of a kale side dish, salad, pasta or fish over kale. With the oil, you could also toss them into a small skillet to lightly brown the crumbs.

TECHNIQUES
Mincing Garlic

There is a difference between chopping garlic and mincing garlic. In my opinion (really my preference), garlic in a dish should blend right in without any garlic pieces being prominent. Especially in a kale sauté, it's nice if the garlic almost disappears in the olive oil, the flavor dispersing. That's why I use the term "finely minced" garlic. To mince the garlic finely you can either use a garlic press, which I often do for ease, or really chop the garlic until it is mashed to nearly a paste. Add some salt while you are chopping—that helps draw out moisture—and just keep chopping.

Making Croutons

Homemade croutons add great flavor and satisfying crunch and are especially nice with kale salads. Kale is rather soft, and benefits occasionally from a nice crunch.

1 medium-size Italian, French, or sourdough loaf, crusts removed, cubed (about 3 cups)

2 tablespoons olive oil

1 teaspoon finely minced garlic

Salt and freshly ground black pepper

1. Preheat the oven to 350°F. Place the bread cubes in a bowl and toss them with the olive oil and garlic; season with salt and pepper.

2. Place the cubes on a baking sheet and toast them in the oven for 10 to 12 minutes, or until the bread is slightly crisp and brown but still soft on the inside.

Note: You can substitute 1 tablespoon of melted butter for 1 tablespoon of the olive oil. You can also toss in chopped fresh herbs, such as parsley or rosemary.

Toasting Nuts

The flavor of most nuts and seeds intensifies when they're toasted, especially walnuts, pecans, sliced almonds, hazelnuts, cashews and sesame seeds. I like pine nuts either way, toasted or untoasted. Because kale, cooked or in salads, has a soft texture, it benefits greatly from the crunch and taste of nuts.

Preheat the oven or toaster oven to 350°F. Place the nuts on a baking sheet and bake until lightly toasted and fragrant, usually 6 to 9 minutes, depending on the kind of nut or seed. Remove from the oven and let cool. Take care to avoid burning the nuts, which can happen very quickly, and use a timer, because it's easy to forget. By the time you smell the nuts, they're usually burned.

Hard-boiling an Egg

This method seems to work easily every time. Place any amount of eggs in a saucepan large enough for a single layer, and fill two-thirds to three-quarters full of cold water. Bring to a boil, then turn off the heat, cover the pan with a lid and set a timer for 10 minutes. Then lift the eggs from the hot water and cool under running cold water or in a bowl filled with cold water before peeling. One science-based cooking site, which also uses this same technique, discovered that the right amount of water to use here is 1½ quarts (for one to six large eggs).

One note of caution, very fresh farm eggs—which are readily available these days—might be more difficult to peel. Try to use eggs that are a few days old, for easier peeling.

Dicing a Mango

Remove the mango skin with a paring knife or Y-shaped peeler. Slice a little off the larger end of the mango so you can hold the fruit upright. Cut slices about ¼ inch thick down on either side of the pit. You should get two or three slices, depending on the mango size. Cut each slice into ¼-inch strips, and each strip into ¼-inch dice.

Opening a Pomegranate

The colors of red pomegranate seeds with kale looks fantastic, and I had to stop myself from adding them to all kinds of salads and kale dishes. And there's an easy method for opening the fruit.

Over the years I've tried many different methods suggested for opening a pomegranate, but the best one came from Abe, an employee at my local Whole Foods Market who originally hails from Egypt. With a paring knife, cut a circle the size of a quarter around the top and bottom ends of the pomegranate and remove each circle. Use the knife to score the fruit on the outside in four equal quarters, just cutting through the thin red peel, not through to the seeds. Open the fruit into quarters, and remove the seeds from each quarter over a bowl. Discard any white pith.

Pomegranate season seems to stretch longer and longer each year, but it's primarily a fall–early winter fruit.

Making Pizza Dough

This recipe can be made ahead and stored for two to three days in the refrigerator or frozen. You can also double the recipe.

1 (1¼-ounce) package active dry yeast
¼ cup warm water (110° to 115°F)
3 cups unbleached all-purpose flour, plus more as needed
2 teaspoons kosher salt
1½ tablespoons olive oil, plus more for bowl
¾ cup plus 2 tablespoons cool water

USING A STANDING MIXER

1. In a small bowl, stir the yeast into the warm water. Let stand for 5 minutes, or until foamy.

2. In the bowl of a standing mixer fitted with a dough hook, combine the 3 cups of flour and the salt and mix. Add the yeast mixture, olive oil and cool water. On low speed, mix until an elastic dough forms, 4 to 5 minutes. (If the dough is rough and sticky, not satiny, add a bit more flour; if the dough is crumbly and not coming together, add additional water, 1 tablespoon at a time.) Finish kneading briefly by hand on a lightly floured counter, 1 minute.

3. Place the dough in a lightly oiled bowl covered with a clean, damp kitchen towel and let it rise in a warm spot until doubled in size, about 1 hour.

4. Place a little flour on your hands, and cut or tear the dough in two. Roll each piece into a ball, and then stretch the top of the ball down around the sides to the bottom to make a tight outer skin. Pinch the bottom together. Cover the pizza balls with a damp towel and let rest for 15 to 20 minutes. At this point, the dough can be rolled out for a pizza or placed in a plastic bag and stored in the refrigerator for 2 or 3 days or in the freezer.

MIXING BY HAND

1. In a small bowl, stir the yeast into the warm water. Let stand for 5 minutes, until foamy. In a large bowl, combine the 3 cups of flour and the salt and mix. Add the yeast mixture, olive oil and cool water. Mix with a wooden spoon until the dough comes together.

2. Flour your hands and knead the ball on a lightly floured counter for about 5 minutes.

3. Place in an oiled bowl and follow step 3 above to raise the dough and make the balls.

Making Tomato Sauce for Pizza or Calzones

You can make a double batch of sauce, freeze it and have sauce ready for the next pizza fest.

2 tablespoons extra-virgin olive oil

2 garlic cloves, finely minced

1 (28-ounce) can whole tomatoes, juices drained, chopped or pulsed 4 times in a food processor

Pinch of sugar

2 teaspoons dried oregano

¼ teaspoon salt, or more to taste

¼ cup fresh basil, slivered (optional)

1. Heat the olive oil in a medium-size, thick-bottomed saucepan on medium-low heat. Add the garlic and sizzle for 1 to 2 minutes. Add the tomatoes, sugar and oregano.

2. Turn the heat to high and when the sauce begins to bubble, lower the heat to low and simmer, uncovered, for 10 minutes. Season with salt and add the basil, if using.

Roasting Split Chicken Breasts

Roasting split breasts (bone-in, with skin) provides moist, tender chicken in 35 to 40 minutes. Preheat the oven to 350°F. Place the split breasts on a rimmed cookie sheet lined with parchment paper for easy cleanup. Brush or rub both sides with olive oil and sprinkle generously with salt. Roast for 35 to 40 minutes, or slightly longer for very large pieces, until the chicken registers 160°F on an instant-read thermometer. You can also check for doneness by making a small cut with a knife. When the meat turns from pink to white, the chicken is done.

THE RECIPES

Breakfast

Kale Granola

The combination of kale, oats and nuts is crunchy and satisfying. Everyone likes to munch on this as a snack—it doesn't even seem to last until breakfast to top yogurt, mix with fruit or serve with milk. It's easy to vary the nuts and the dried fruit with your favorites.

5   cups curly kale (stripped from stalk, chopped or torn into large bite-size pieces, rinsed and dried well)

6   tablespoons virgin coconut oil, divided (see cook's note)

¾   teaspoon kosher salt

¼   cup light brown sugar

6   tablespoons pure maple syrup

3   cups rolled oats

1   cup broken pecans, broken walnuts or sliced almonds

½   cup sunflower seeds

¼   cup sesame seeds

1   cup dried cranberries, roughly chopped

¼   cup dried apricots, chopped into ¼-inch pieces

¼   cup raisins, roughly chopped

1.   Preheat the oven to 300°F.

2.   Make sure the kale is well dried. Place the kale in a bowl with 1 tablespoon of the coconut oil and ¼ teaspoon of the salt. Knead or massage with your hands until the coconut oil is rubbed on all the leaves. Set aside.

3.   In a small bowl, whisk together the remaining 5 tablespoons of coconut oil, and the brown sugar, maple syrup and remaining ½ teaspoon of salt. In another, larger bowl, combine the oats, nuts and seeds.

4.   Take 2 tablespoons of the wet ingredients and combine with the kale. Rub it over the leaves. Pour the rest over the oat mixture and mix very well until incorporated and the oats are completely covered.

5.   Line two 12 x 17-inch baking sheets with parchment paper or a silicone mat. Place the oats on one sheet, spreading them out evenly, and the kale on the other sheet. (The kale seems to crisp up better separately, but you can mix the kale and oats together and it will work.) Bake all for 25 to 30 minutes, mixing two or three times to prevent the outer edges from burning, and also rotating the pans. I sometimes switch the oven setting to CONVECTION BAKE if the mixture doesn't seem to be crisping up. Remove the kale when it is crispy, but not browned. Remove the oats when they are crispy or nearly crispy and before the nuts are burned. Both will get crispier once they sit on the counter to cool.

6.   When cooled, combine the kale with the oats. Add the dried fruit. Pack into mason jars for storage.

Cook's Note: I've switched to coconut oil instead of canola oil for making granola (though, substitute canola or another vegetable oil if that is what you have). I love the subtle flavor coconut adds, and nutritionists are recommending its healthier properties. In warmer weather, coconut oil looks like an oil; in cooler weather it tends to solidify. For this recipe, if it has solidified, I usually put the jar in a saucepan of hot water until it becomes liquid again. Also, if you mix it with cold maple syrup it tends to solidify again, which makes it hard to coat the oats and kale, so I usually just have the syrup at room temperature or heat it up very slightly before mixing the liquid ingredients.

Egg and Kale Breakfast Burritos

These kid-friendly burritos combine scrambled eggs with colorful vegetables and a bit of cheese. Choose a few toppings—avocado, chopped tomato, cilantro, additional cheese or salsa—to place in small bowls to accompany. Place everything on the table and let everyone assemble their own. Because the kale is sautéed with the veggies, try a kale that will tenderize easily when sautéed, such as Italian, Red Russian or younger kale.

4	large flour tortillas
1	tablespoon olive oil
2	scallions, white and light green parts, chopped (about ¼ cup)
1	red bell pepper, cored and diced small (about ¾ cup)
3	cups lacinato or Red Russian kale, stripped from stalk, chopped into ½-inch pieces, rinsed and dried)
6	eggs
2	tablespoons water
¼	teaspoon salt, or more to taste
4–5	drops hot sauce, or more to taste
1	cup shredded Monterey Jack, pepper Jack or Cheddar cheese
½	avocado, pitted and diced
1	small tomato, chopped
	Your favorite salsa

1. Preheat the oven to 300°F. Wrap the tortillas in foil and place in the oven to warm.

2. In a large skillet, preferably nonstick, heat the olive oil on medium-high heat and sauté the scallions, red pepper and kale together for 4 to 5 minutes, until the kale is tender. Use tongs to continually toss the mixture in the hot skillet, like stir-frying. Transfer to a bowl and set aside.

3. Whisk the eggs, water and the ¼ teaspoon of salt together in a bowl. Wipe out the skillet, add a film of oil and scramble the eggs on medium-low heat. When the eggs are done, add the hot sauce and/or additional salt to taste, the cheese and the kale mixture. Stir gently until reheated.

4. Place the skillet on the table, along with the tortillas. Accompany with bowls of chopped avocado, chopped tomato and salsa.

Raw Kale Salad with Fruit and Nuts

This is a juicy way to spice up kale in any season, as well as a good salad for a brunch or potluck. Feel free to mix up the fruit, substitute fresh pineapple or mango, or add a few tablespoons of fresh mint.

- 6 cups kale (about 1 bunch, stripped from stalk, chopped into bite-size pieces, rinsed and dried well)
- 2 teaspoons olive oil
- 2 pinches of kosher salt
- ⅓ cup unsweetened shredded coconut, lightly toasted
- ½ cup dried apricots, thinly sliced or diced
- 1½ cups fresh blueberries
- 1–2 oranges, outside peel removed with a serrated knife, orange sliced into rounds and cut into half-moons
- 1 tart apple, cored and diced
- ½ cup sliced almonds, toasted

LEMON DRESSING

- 2 tablespoons fresh lemon juice
- 6 tablespoons olive oil
- 2 pinches of salt

1. Add the olive oil and salt to the kale and massage with your hands until all the leaves are coated, 2 to 3 minutes. The kale will reduce in volume somewhat and taste good.

2. Make the dressing: Whisk together the lemon juice and olive oil. Season with the salt.

3. Place the kale in a wide bowl or platter. Dress the kale with most of the dressing and mix well. Mix in half of the coconut. Top with the apricots, blueberries, orange slices and apple. Drizzle the rest of the dressing on top. Garnish with the rest of the coconut and the almonds.

THE KALE CHRONICLES

Eggs and Kale Are Really Good Together

It was time to retest a recipe titled "Black Beans and Kale with a Fried Egg," which I had made a month or two earlier.

In my notes, I described this recipe as "a fairly easy breakfast." So, I started it one school morning twenty minutes before James was going to take his bus to school. This would be a good test.

This thought did cross my mind: "Would I be making a kale dish at six thirty in the morning if I weren't writing this book?"

I cooked the kale, sautéed garlic and added canned black beans along with a little chili powder. I fried an egg to go on top. It's supposed to go atop a flour or corn tortilla, which I thought I had but didn't. Instead, I put it on a few thin slices of uncured salami. A squeeze of lime juice and some diced avocado, a quick grating of Cheddar cheese and it was done.

I was half expecting a grimace from James—I was serving him black beans and kale on a Wednesday morning before school. He ate away. "How is it?" I asked.

"It's good," he said, not looking up at me.

The scene was nearly identical when I served it to Dave. "This is good," he said.

After I had finished my coffee, showered and dressed, I was finally ready to eat. I heated up the kale and fried myself an egg. A little squeeze of lime juice on top of the diced avocado. I wasn't sure I was up for it—I'm generally a coffee-and-piece-of-toast person. Lately, I can't get enough of the kale smoothies I've been testing.

But one bite, and it clicked. Eggs and kale taste delicious together. The runny warm yolk spilling onto the mixture, little bites of beans and cheese, cilantro and lime. It worked, and it was fairly easy.

Over time, I have served eggs and kale in multiple combination—in a frittata, in a breakfast burrito with scrambled eggs, as poached eggs over kale with an easy hollandaise sauce, and in a number of other breakfast (or dinner) dishes.

My friend Mary Estella showed me her easy kale and egg dish—Paleo style—the night I stayed at her house on a business trip. In a medium-size saucepan, she boils a cup or two of water, adds whole kale leaves (minus the stems) and lets them cook for three to four minutes. Then she poaches one or two eggs on top of the kale leaves: she puts in the egg, covers the pot, and in two to three minutes, breakfast is ready. She lifts out the egg-topped kale with a flat strainer, and adds a pinch of salt and a squirt of olive oil.

But my favorite discovery while writing this book was cracking the eggs right in a pan over a mix of onion, sausage, tomatoes and kale. I had gotten the idea from a photo in the book *Plenty*, by Yotam Ottolenghi. I don't even recall the ingredients, beyond the four eggs that were beautifully cooked sitting on top of what looked like roasted peppers, tomato and fresh green herbs. I tried it with tomatoes and kale from the garden, local sausage from the farmers' market and some feta cheese. I cracked four eggs on top, kept the pan on medium heat, added a cover, and in minutes, the eggs were cooked. A beautiful dish of eggs for four.

All because of kale.

Egg and Kale Casserole

This is the easiest egg and kale dish made in our kitchen in which nothing needs to be sautéed ahead of time. It's especially good to use up ingredients you might already have on hand, such as bacon, ham, sausage, cooked potatoes, tomatoes, even leftover cooked kale.

- 3 cups kale (stripped from stalk, chopped into bite-size pieces and rinsed)
- 6 eggs
- ½ cup milk
- ½ teaspoon salt
- 1 cup grated Cheddar cheese

1. Preheat the oven to 350°F. Oil or butter an 8 x 8-inch glass baking dish. Precook the kale in 2 cups of boiling water, covered, for about 4 minutes. Drain, shake the strainer to cool, and when cool, squeeze out any excess moisture. Set aside.

2. Whisk the eggs and milk together in a bowl. Add the salt.

3. Place the kale in the prepared baking dish. Top with the cheese. Pour the egg mixture on top and mix slightly with a fork to evenly distribute the kale.

4. Bake for 25 to 30 minutes, until the eggs are set.

Baked Eggs, Kale and Feta

Serve this easy dish for breakfast, brunch or dinner, with a leafy green salad or kale salad. I like using a glass pie dish for baking because the pie-shaped wedges look nice on a plate with a salad.

- 1 tablespoon olive oil or butter
- 1 medium-size onion, diced small (about 1 cup)
- 2 garlic cloves, finely minced
- ⅛ teaspoon crushed red pepper flakes
- 2 cups kale (stripped from stalk, chopped into small pieces and rinsed)
- 5 eggs
- ½ cup milk, half-and-half or cream
- ½ teaspoon kosher salt
-   Freshly ground black pepper
- 1 cup feta cheese (sheep's milk or sheep's/goat's milk make it more flavorful)
- 6–8 cherry tomatoes, quartered (optional, for color)

1. Preheat the oven to 350°F. Heat the olive oil in a large skillet and sauté the onion until translucent, about 5 minutes, stirring often. Add the garlic and red pepper flakes and sauté for another 30 seconds, until fragrant. Add the kale and sauté on medium heat until tender, about 5 more minutes, stirring often. Add a bit of water, if the mixture is sticking.

2. Whisk the eggs together in a bowl. Add the milk, salt and pepper. Crumble the feta and mix in along with the kale mixture. Pour into a 9-inch glass pie dish or square baking dish. Bake for 30 to 35 minutes, until puffed and the filling is set.

3. If using the cherry tomatoes, let the dish bake for about 15 minutes before adding the tomatoes on top, so they don't sink.

4. Slice and serve immediately. Slices do reheat nicely in a microwave.

Breakfast Eggs, Sausage and Kale

This is a nice Sunday dish with breakfast meat, eggs and kale all cooked in the same skillet. After the sausage and onions are cooked and combined with some tomatoes, the eggs are nestled on top and poached right in the pan. A flavorful sausage is helpful to the overall taste. I've had luck with the local farm sausages, which I've found delicious and not that fatty.

- 1   tablespoon olive oil
- 1   onion, thinly sliced
-     Salt
- ½   pound pork sausage (mild Italian or another flavor), removed from casing
- 1   tablespoon finely minced garlic
- 1   (28-ounce) can diced tomatoes, with juices
- 1   tablespoon chopped fresh oregano, or 2 teaspoons dried
- 4   cups kale (about 8 ounces, stripped from stalk, chopped into bite-size pieces, rinsed and dried)
- 4   eggs
- ½   cup feta cheese

1. In a large sauté pan with a lid, heat the olive oil and sauté the onion over medium heat for 8 to 10 minutes, until starting to soften and turn golden. Add a pinch of salt. Add the sausage, breaking it up as it cooks, stirring the mixture constantly, about 5 minutes. (A wooden spoon with a flat end works great to break up any clumps of sausage as they cook.) Add the garlic; stir for a minute. Add the tomatoes, oregano and two pinches of salt and simmer for about 5 minutes, covered.

2. Meanwhile, bring a saucepan of 3 to 4 cups of water to a boil. Add the kale and boil, covered, for 5 minutes, or until tender. Drain, and set aside.

3. When the tomato mixture has simmered, mix in the kale. Gently break each egg on top of the mixture, leaving space between the eggs. Cover, and very gently simmer on low heat until the eggs are cooked, 5 to 7 minutes. Sprinkle the feta on top. Place the sauté pan at the table and let people serve themselves. Serve immediately.

Black Beans and Kale with a Fried Egg

Serve this for a fairly easy breakfast or dinner—the kale is quickly combined with black beans sautéed with a little garlic and chili powder. It can be served over a corn or flour tortilla, thin slices of Italian cured meats, sausage or bacon, or even on its own. Don't forget a little diced avocado and a squeeze of lime juice—a small burst of flavor at the end. You can easily cut this recipe in half for two people.

- 3 cups kale (stripped from stalk, chopped into small bite-size pieces and rinsed)
- 1 tablespoon olive oil
- 2 teaspoons finely minced garlic (about 3 cloves)
- 2 teaspoons chili powder
- 1 (14-ounce) can black beans, drained and rinsed
- 4 eggs
- 1 cup grated Cheddar cheese
- Salt
- 4 corn or wheat tortillas (optional)
- ½ avocado, pitted and diced
- 2 lime wedges
- Cilantro leaves, for garnish (optional)

1. Bring at least 3 cups of water to a boil in a medium or large skillet and add the kale. Cover and cook over high heat until tender, 4 to 5 minutes, stirring occasionally. Strain in a colander, and shake several times to release the steam.

2. Wipe out the skillet, and heat the olive oil over medium-low heat. Add the garlic and chili powder and sauté for a minute or less, stirring to prevent the garlic from burning. Add the black beans, and a few tablespoons of water, if needed. Add the kale, most of the cheese and a few pinches of salt and mix well.

3. Heat a nonstick pan, and warm the tortillas, if using. (Alternatively, you can heat the tortillas in the oven or microwave.) Set aside. Fry the eggs, one at a time.

4. To serve, place a tortilla, if using, on a plate, and top with the kale mixture, then the fried egg, or serve the egg-topped kale directly on the plate. Add a squeeze of lime juice, a bit more shredded cheese and diced avocado. Garnish with cilantro, if desired.

Rachel and Finn's Coconut Kale Smoothie MAKES 16 OUNCES (1 OR 2 SERVINGS)

Rachel, a friend and private chef from Montana and Martha's Vineyard, says this kale smoothie is her son Finn's favorite. Coconut crystals are gaining in popularity as a sweetener for having nearly half the glycemic index of sugar, as well as minerals, including potassium, magnesium, calcium and zinc.

1	cup coconut, almond or cow's milk
½	cup ice
1	frozen ripe banana
1	tablespoon coconut crystals or other sweetener
1	kale leaf, stripped from stalk, chopped and rinsed
½	cup spinach leaves, well rinsed
3	sprigs fresh parsley
3	sprigs fresh cilantro
1	tablespoon fresh lemon juice

OPTIONAL ADD-INS

1	tablespoon protein powder
½	avocado, pitted

Place all the ingredients in a blender and blend from low to high speed until smooth. Add additional water or ice if too thick.

Variations: Try this with fresh mango, or mango and pineapple—so delicious.

Blueberry Watermelon Blast

In the heat of summer, these cooling smoothies are great for a breakfast or lunch you can make in a blender. The watermelon adds a hint of sweetness and the avocado makes it creamy. But the color stays an appealing dark blue from the blueberries.

  1   cup fresh watermelon, seeded
  1   cup frozen blueberries
 1½   cups kale (stripped from stalks, chopped and rinsed)
  ½   avocado, pitted
  1   cup water (or ice if using fresh blueberries)
  1   teaspoon fresh lemon juice

Place all the ingredients in a blender. Blend from low to high speed until smooth and creamy.

Peach Smoothie

MAKES 16 OUNCES (1 OR 2 SERVINGS)

This is a light and frothy breakfast, with three servings of vegetables, three servings of fruit, plus yogurt.

  1   cup frozen sliced peaches
  1   banana
  ⅓   cup plain yogurt
  1   cup water
 1½   cups baby kale (stemmed, chopped and rinsed)

Place the peaches, banana, yogurt and water in a blender. Blend from low to high speed. Add the kale and blend again until green specks appear.

Tropical Mango, Orange and Kale Smoothie

This is a favorite kale smoothie. Perfect for a quick breakfast or snack.

1½ cups kale or baby kale (stripped from stalk, chopped and rinsed)

1 ripe mango, peeled, pitted and cut into chunks (for how to peel a mango, see page 46)

2 oranges, peeled, sliced and seeded

½ cup water

1 banana

3 pitted dried dates

1 cup ice

Place all the ingredients in a blender. Blend from low to high speed until creamy and smooth. Add additional water if needed.

Kale Pineapple Smoothie

MAKES 16 OUNCES (1 OR 2 SERVINGS)

Pineapple and banana make a kale smoothie delicious tasting—almost like having a dessert for breakfast or lunch.

1½ cups kale or baby kale (stripped from stalk, chopped and rinsed)

1 cup fresh pineapple chunks, and any juice

4 pitted dried dates

1 banana

1 cup ice

1½ cups water

OPTIONAL ADD-INS

1 tablespoon ground flaxseed

1 tablespoon unsweetened shredded coconut

Place the ingredients in a blender. Blend from low to high speed until smooth and creamy.

Berry Kalicious

For a "green" smoothie, this fruit and kale breakfast drink has a brilliant blue color from the blueberries, and added flavor from strawberries and raspberries. The dates add a touch of sweetness and blend right in.

- 1 cup frozen blueberries
- ½ cup frozen strawberries
- ½ cup frozen raspberries
- 7 pitted dates
- 1½ cups kale or baby kale (stripped from stalk, chopped and rinsed)
- 1½ cups water

Place all the ingredients in a blender and blend from low to high speed until smooth. Add an additional ¼ cup of water if too thick.

Eric's Ultimate Kale Smoothie

My friend Eric Pyenson developed this smoothie as a postworkout restorative. It also works as the healthy person's version of a liquid lunch. It took some time, and several iterations, before Eric got the recipe from what he calls "primordial sludge" to this delicious drink. Even his wife, food writer and cookbook author Andrea Pyenson, now finds herself craving it.

- 1 cup fresh orange juice
- 3 large leaves of green kale, stripped from stalk and rinsed
- 2 carrots, peeled
- 2 celery stalks
- 1 (1½-inch piece) fresh ginger, peeled and sliced into coins
- 1 apple, cored and quartered
- 1 clementine or tangerine, peeled and seeded
- 1½ lemon, peeled and seeded
- 2 tablespoons honey or thyme honey
- 2 handfuls of ice cubes

Place the orange juice in a blender or Vitamix, followed by all the other ingredients, except the ice. Blend on medium speed until integrated. Add the ice and blend on high speed for an additional minute. Pour and enjoy!

Cook's Note: For added creaminess, add ½ avocado, pitted, and ¼ cup plain Greek yogurt before blending.

Strawberry Banana Kale Smoothie

MAKES 16 OUNCES (1 OR 2 SERVINGS)

If you blend in the kale at the end, the smoothie stays a nice pink color with flecks of green. This is my son's favorite kale smoothie.

- 1 cup frozen strawberries
- 1 cup fresh squeezed orange juice or water, or more if needed
- 1 large banana
- ½ cup plain yogurt
- 1 cup kale (stripped from stalk, chopped and rinsed)

Place the strawberries, orange juice, banana and yogurt in a blender and blend from low to high speed until creamy. Add the kale and blend until you see very small green specks and the smoothie is still strawberry pink. Add water, if needed.

Summer Sunrise Smoothie

MAKES 16 OUNCES (1 OR 2 SERVINGS)

A healthier orange juice for the summer, especially if you have some extra watermelon in the fridge. The watermelon and banana add a touch of sweetness to this light and refreshing smoothie, a perfect partner for kale in the morning, or for a pick-me-up snack.

- 2 cups watermelon, seeded
- 1 cup frozen raspberries
- 1 banana
- ½ cup fresh squeezed orange juice (2 juice oranges)
- 1 tablespoon fresh lime juice
- 1½ cups kale (stripped from stalk, chopped and rinsed

Place all the ingredients, except the kale, in a blender. Blend from low to high speed until the raspberry seeds are unnoticeable. Add the kale and blend until it has nearly disappeared but the smoothie is still a nice pinkish-red color from the watermelon and raspberries.

Crispy Kale Chips

I think one of the keys to getting crispy kale chips is to give the kale a good massage, to produce an even coating of olive oil before baking. Also, use a pair of tongs to mix the kale at least once while in the oven. If a few pieces look like they might burn before the rest is done, transfer them to the serving bowl, and let the rest finish. The kale seems to get crisper as well as it cools on the baking sheet.

6–8 cups kale (about 1 bunch)
   1 tablespoon olive oil
      Salt

1. Preheat the oven to 300°F.
2. Strip the kale from the ribs. Tear into large pieces, about 1½ to 2 inches. Fill a salad spinner with water, swish the kale around and spin dry. Make sure the kale is as dry as possible.
3. Place the kale in a bowl and drizzle with the olive oil and two pinches of salt. Massage the oil into all parts of the kale.
4. Divide between two baking sheets and bake for about 20 minutes, or until crispy. Mix once or twice while baking. To ensure crispiness without burning, near the end of cooking, you can remove the chips that are crispy, and return the baking sheet to the oven to let the remaining pieces get crispy.

Variation: Lemon-Pepper Kale Chips: When the kale chips are removed from the oven, grind a bit of fresh pepper on top and add a few drops of fresh lemon juice.

Fresh Kale and Vegetable Spring Rolls

Light, refreshing and full of veggies and kale, these spring rolls will disappear quickly. Serve on mini-appetizer or salad plates with a prepared sweet chili sauce or homemade peanut sauce, so people can dip in their own sauce before each bite. Any type of kale will work here—curly, lacinato or Red Russian. These are best made and consumed on the same day.

5   cups kale (stripped from stalk, chopped into small bite-size pieces, rinsed and dried)

1   tablespoon olive oil

½   teaspoon salt

5   cups cooked and rinsed rice vermicelli (see cook's note)

2   cups shredded carrot (2 to 3 carrots)

¾   cup chopped fresh cilantro leaves

1   cup fresh mint leaves, thinly sliced or chopped, but not minced

1½ cups cucumber (about 1 large cucumber, peeled, seeded and cut into tiny dice)

1   cup unsalted peanuts, chopped (pulsing in food processor works well)

1   (12-ounce) package (8- or 9-inch) round or square rice spring roll wrappers

Sweet chili sauce (such as Maesri or Mae Ploy brand) or peanut dipping sauce

1. Place the kale in a large mixing bowl. Add the olive oil and salt and, with your hands, massage the kale, rubbing the oil and salt into all the pieces for 2 to 3 minutes. The kale will reduce in volume, turn a dark green and soften. You should have about 4 cups.

2. Chop the cooked, rinsed noodles a little to make them more manageable and add to the kale. Mix well, separating the kale and noodles to integrate. Add the carrot, cilantro, mint, cucumber and peanuts.

3. To soften the wrappers, fill a skillet with water and bring to a boil. Turn off the heat, and then reheat as needed. Wet a clean dish towel, wring out and place on a cutting board to place rice paper on.

4. Dip one rice paper wrapper in the hot water, making sure it's submerged. When softened, 5 to 10 seconds, transfer the wrapper to the dish towel.

5. Spread about ½ cup of the filling on the bottom third of the wrapper. Starting with the end closest to you, roll the wrapper tightly around the filling. When it's rolled halfway up, fold the sides of the wrapper toward the center and continue rolling to the end of the wrapper. Continue until all the filling is wrapped.

6. Place on a baking sheet and cover with plastic wrap to keep the rolls from drying out. They can be made up to 3 hours ahead, the tray covered with its plastic wrap and stored in the fridge. Serve with the sweet chili sauce.

Cook's Note: Cooking rice noodles properly is just like making regular pasta. Boil them in a pot of salted water and taste until the noodles are the right consistency, a bit al dente. The big difference is timing; typically the rice stick vermicelli might take only 2 to 3 minutes. After straining, run cool water over the noodles to stop the cooking. I sometimes add some sesame oil to keep them from sticking, and for the flavor.

Kale Guacamole

A chunky guacamole with diced avocado, tomato and finely chopped, massaged kale with a bit of heat and fresh lemon or lime juice. It tastes as good as it looks! Make this only an hour or two before serving, so the avocado stays bright.

- 2   cups kale (stripped from stalk, chopped into ¼-inch pieces, rinsed and dried)
- 2   teaspoons olive oil
-     Salt
- 2–3 just-ripe avocados, pitted and cut into ¼-inch dice
- 1   cup tomato (seeded and cut into a small dice)
- 2   tablespoons minced red onion
- 4   teaspoons fresh lemon or lime juice (or a combination)
- ½   teaspoon ground cumin
- ⅛   teaspoon smoked paprika or cayenne pepper

1. Place the kale in a medium-size bowl. Drizzle with the olive oil and two pinches of salt and massage the kale by rubbing the oil onto the kale until it's reduced in size a bit and glistening. If it releases moisture, soak it up with a paper towel. If the pieces are too large, chop again with a knife.

2. Add the avocados, tomato, red onion, lemon juice, cumin, paprika and two more pinches of salt. Toss gently—it's nice to keep the avocado separate rather than mashed together. Taste with a chip to make sure you have the right amount of salt and citrus. Place in a serving dish, surrounded by corn tortilla chips.

Cook's Note: You might see me at the supermarket, lingering at the avocado bin, trying to find that perfect just-ripe avocado. Buying an avocado is like buying a watermelon or melon—you never know exactly what you'll get inside. I avoid rock hard or the soft avocados. I use my thumb to press gently into the avocado. If it indents slightly it will usually be all green inside without brown spots—just right. My friend Molly says her trick is to remove the tiny stem cap at the top of the avocado. If it's bright green underneath the cap, she finds it's usually bright green inside without brown spots.

THE KALE CHRONICLES

Kale Chip Origins

Who created the first kale chip?

I know it wasn't me, unfortunately. When Johnna Albi and I wrote *Greens, Glorious Greens* in 1996, kale chips or crispy kale did not exist. We spent a year researching, eating and writing about leafy greens including kale—nary a word or recipe. Now kale chips are a household word, and probably have done more to increase the popularity of kale than anything else. This snack could even be the reason there is a current worldwide shortage of kale seeds.

I've always credited the discovery of kale chips with Joanie Ames, here on Martha's Vineyard. She first brought crispy kale chips to a Slow Food potluck in around 2006. The dish caught our attention, as people admired the crunch and saltiness. The fact it was kale—a green vegetable—as easily consumed as a bag of potato chips or cheese puffs made an impact. Was this a truly healthy snack?

Soon, kale chips spread like wildfire around the island. They appeared—and were happily consumed—at nearly every potluck. I'd overhear conversations about the best roasting temperature for the crispiest kale. Was it low—275°F, as Joanie first recommended—or the higher 350° or 375°F that many found perfectly adequate?

When I printed the recipe in *Martha's Vineyard* magazine in the 2006/2007 winter issue, Joanie got the credit, as I had never seen another recipe for this. But somehow, the practice became ubiquitous across the country. I believe the kale roasting method was shared in other communities in similar patterns—by way of word of mouth. Every article or blog I've read started with, "I recently sampled kale chips at my [cousin's brother's friend's] house."

When I recently asked Joanie again about how she started, she said she first learned the technique from her nephew's wife, Elise Hoblitzelle of Watertown, Massachusetts. That was in 2005. "I just thought they were remarkable," Joanie says. "So I worked with the recipe for a while and tried different oven temperatures, only salting them lightly after they'd been kneaded with olive oil." Joanie settled on 300°F. She also suggests removing the kale pieces that are really crispy so they don't burn. "You have to watch them like a baby—they go from being still green and crispy, which is the way you want them, to going just brown."

She, herself, finds the rapid-fire dissemination amazing, all the way to the delicious, commercially made chocolate-coated kale her daughter gave her over the holidays. "Whoever thought it would go that far and that fast? It makes you realize how connected we all are."

Eventually, recipes appeared everywhere, and many got creative with the basic kale chip recipe that uses kale, olive oil and salt. Food Network personality Guy Fiori adds crushed red pepper and a squeeze of lemon after roasting. Another Food Network host, Jeff Mauro, bakes BBQ kale chips with paprika, ancho chili powder and brown sugar. Cookbook author Ellie Krieger's smoked kale chips are made with a dusting of smoked paprika.

When I reached Elise Hoblitzelle, Joanie's source, about creating the kale chips, she said she had not previously seen a recipe for them when she first started making them around 2004, when her son was about six.

"We had friends who were grilling [kale]. We loved that. I wanted to figure out how to do a similar thing in the winter," explains Elise, who said after stripping kale from the spine and tearing it into pieces she massaged them altogether with salt and olive oil before popping into a 350°F oven. "I feel like I adapted the grilled kale and started making it in the oven. I remember telling friends about it and they were wild about it."

In the larger world, credit seems to go elsewhere.

Maine historian and author Sandy Oliver, who researches the history of New England foods, especially fish and shellfish, wondered whether kale chips could be considered a historical trend that would withstand the test of time or simply be as she says, a "blip on the radar of time."

Oliver first discovered kale chips herself from a "neighbor," and it caught her attention—both the chip itself and the phenomenon. As a researcher, she began to look into the subject and came up with a date of 2005 for kale chips, attributed to one of the local food movement pioneers, Dan Barber, the chef at Blue Hill restaurant at Stone Barns in New York.

In 2009, *Bon Appétit* printed Chef Barber's recipe for kale chips. That prominent placement help kale chips—and kale itself—take off. A 2013 *Time* magazine article about Barber dubbed him the "King of Kale." I did track down Chef Barber's e-mail from a colleague, but he failed to respond to the two e-mails I sent inquiring whether in fact he created the recipe on his own or saw it somewhere first.

In my own research, I found a reference to kale chips as far back as 2004—the year Elise was testing them—at a website called Radical Health, featuring raw foods. Instead of the kale's being baked in the oven, it was crisped in a dehydrator.

Did Elise and Dan and the guy from Radical Health all start creating kale chips simultaneously, or was one of them—or even someone else—responsible for the very first chip? I'm still curious, and will go on with the research. Meanwhile, I'll continue to enjoy this uniquely delicious snack, grateful that someone started the ball rolling, even if it wasn't me.

Maple-Sesame Kale Chips

Just a tad of sweetness from maple syrup and crunch from sesame seeds for this addictive healthy snack.

5 cups kale (stripped from stalk, torn into pieces a little larger than bite-size, rinsed and dried)

1 tablespoon olive oil

2 pinches of salt

2 tablespoons pure maple syrup

⅛ teaspoon cayenne pepper

3 tablespoons sesame seeds

1. Preheat the oven to 300°F. Place the kale in a large bowl and drizzle with the olive oil and two pinches of salt. Massage the kale with your hands until all areas of the kale leaves are covered and softened a bit. Mix in the maple syrup, cayenne and sesame seeds. Most of the sesame seeds should stick to the leaves.

2. Place on a parchment paper–lined baking sheet. Bake for 25 to 28 minutes, mixing several times to prevent the outer edges from burning and to keep the kale pieces as separate as possible. Taste a piece while cooking and add an additional pinch of salt, if needed. Let cool on the baking sheet; the mixture should crisp up nicely.

Variation: Add a sheet of nori seaweed to the mix, tearing it up and roasting it in the last few minutes of the baking process.

Olive-Kale Tapenade Spread

The kale enlivens this traditional olive spread with bright green flecks. Because all the ingredients go right into a food processor, this makes a quick and easy appetizer—and a perfect complement to cocktails, adding that salty counterpoint to the alcohol. This tastes delicious with fresh baguette slices, but you can also serve with toast points, crostini or water crackers, or on a cheese platter.

2 small or medium-size garlic cloves

⅔ cup pitted kalamata olives

2 cups kale (stripped from stalk, roughly chopped, rinsed and dried)

5 grinds of black pepper

2 tablespoons olive oil

Kale leaves, for garnish

1. Place the garlic in the food processor first and chop finely. Add the olives, kale, pepper and olive oil and pulse until the mixture reaches a finely chopped consistency. (If you pulse, rather than run, the processor, the mixture gets nicely chopped and both olive black and kale green show distinctively.)

2. Take a small bowl and decorate the inside with kale leaves. Place the tapenade in the bowl.

Roasted Kale, Garlic and Sesame Salt

This condiment is fashioned after gomasio, is a traditional Japanese sesame-salt topping used as a garnish and flavor enhancer for dishes. It's also one way to reduce the use of salt, while adding magnesium, calcium, iron and protein from sesame seeds and kale. This crispy baked kale version is great on vegetables, baked squash, soups, grains, even sautéed kale.

3   cups kale (stripped from stalk, chopped into bite-size pieces, rinsed and dried)

1   tablespoon olive oil

½   teaspoon kosher salt

⅓   cup sesame seeds

1   large garlic clove, finely minced

1. Preheat the oven to 300°F.

2. Line a baking sheet with parchment paper. Place the kale on the baking sheet, and sprinkle with the olive oil and salt. Massage with your hands to coat all parts of the kale leaves with oil and salt. Mix in the sesame seeds and garlic.

3. Bake for 20 to 25 minutes, or until the kale is crispy, but not browned or burned. It will crisp a bit more as it cools. When cooled, break up the kale by rubbing it between your fingers, so the kale is the size of the sesame seeds. Store the mixture in an empty spice container.

Kale and Cheese Quesadillas

West Tisbury elementary school students first taste-tested these quesadillas during a kale cooking class related to their garden program. I figured quesadillas were a good way to get kids to enjoy kale. It worked. Shredded chicken could be added as well. This makes an easy appetizer or dinner. Serve with salsa or guacamole.

½ bunch kale, stripped from stalk, chopped into bite-size pieces and rinsed (about 4 cups)

2 cups shredded cheese (Cheddar, Monterey Jack or a combination)

¼ cup chopped green chiles, found in Mexican section (optional)

1 teaspoon ground cumin

1½ teaspoons chili powder

1 (8- to 10-count) package (8- to 9-inch) flour tortillas

4 teaspoons canola or olive oil

1. Bring 3 to 4 cups of water to a boil in a saucepan. Add the kale and cook on high heat, covered, for 4 to 5 minutes. Drain in a colander; shake several times to help cool. When cool, squeeze out any excess water, and then break any clumps apart.

2. In a large bowl, combine the cheese, green chiles, cumin and chili powder with the kale.

3. Heat an 11- to 12-inch skillet on medium heat, and pour in about 1 teaspoon of canola oil to coat. Place a tortilla in the skillet. Put a generous ½ cup of the cheese mixture in middle of the tortilla. Place another tortilla on top. When the tortilla is lightly browned, flip over. The quesadilla is done when the cheese is melted, 3 to 4 minutes. Repeat for the other quesadillas.

4. Cut into wedges and serve—a pizza cutter works great to cut quesadillas.

Rustic Kale and Goat Cheese Tart

A great appetizer to start a party or serve at a brunch: a flaky crust flavored with a touch of Parmesan cheese and black pepper with a savory filling of Parmesan, goat cheese and kale. You make this easy crust in a food processor. Its rustic look comes from hand molding the crust; no tart pan is needed. It also makes a good accompaniment to soup, as a change from bread.

TART CRUST

- 1¼ cups all-purpose flour
- Pinch of salt
- 2 tablespoons Parmesan cheese
- ¼ teaspoon freshly ground black pepper
- ½ cup (1 stick) butter, cut into small pieces
- 3 tablespoons ice water
- 1 egg, for egg wash

FILLING

- 3 cups kale (about ½ bunch, stripped from stalk, chopped into small pieces but not minced, and rinsed)
- 1 egg
- ⅓ cup ricotta cheese, part-skim or whole milk
- 4 ounces goat cheese (I love the Vermont Butter & Cheese brand)
- ¼ cup Parmigiano-Reggiano cheese
- 1 teaspoon chopped fresh thyme
- 1 tablespoon chopped fresh chives (optional, if available)
- ½ teaspoon kosher salt

1. Make the crust first. Pulse the flour, salt, Parmesan and pepper in a food processor to mix. Add the pieces of butter and pulse until the mixture resembles pebbles. Add the ice water and pulse five or six times to combine. Then run the processor until the dough comes together in a ball. With your hands, form a rough disk and flatten it somewhat. Flour two pieces of parchment or waxed paper and roll out the disk to 12 to 13 inches in diameter. Refrigerate for at least an hour.

2. Preheat the oven to 375°F. Make the filling: In a saucepan, bring 4 cups of water to a boil. Add the kale and cook, covered, on high heat for 4 to 6 minutes, until tender. Drain in a colander and shake to release the steam, to stop the cooking. When cool enough to handle, squeeze out any excess moisture; then break any clumps apart.

3. In a bowl, mix the egg with a fork and add the ricotta, goat cheese, Parmesan, thyme, chives, if using, and salt. Mix well before stirring in the kale.

4. To assemble: Line a baking sheet with a piece of parchment paper and lay the rolled-out dough on top. Run a butter knife around the edges, cutting away a tiny bit of the dough to make it somewhat smooth, rather than ragged. Spread the kale mixture over the dough, leaving a 1-inch border.

5. The dough should be pliable enough at this point to fold without breaking. If so, fold the edges of the dough over onto the mixture, forming pleats every 2 inches or so. Whisk the egg in a small bowl and brush over the dough.

6. Bake for 40 to 45 minutes. About 15 minutes into the baking, take a fork and gently mix the filling. This will prevent the top from browning too much at the end. The tart is done when the crust is golden brown. Serve hot or warm.

Kale and Black Bean Quesadillas

Quesadillas, whether as an appetizer, lunch or main dish, are easy to make and satisfying to eat. Serve as is, or top with guacamole and/or your favorite salsa. Add shredded cooked chicken along with the kale and black beans, if desired.

1	tablespoon olive oil
½	bunch kale, stripped from stalk, chopped into bite-size pieces and rinsed (about 4 cups)
1	cup corn kernels (stripped from 1 ear corn)
2	cups shredded cheese (Cheddar, Monterey Jack, pepper Jack, fontina or a combination)
1	cup canned black beans, drained and rinsed
¼	cup chopped mild green chiles (found in Mexican section)
1	teaspoon ground cumin
1½	teaspoons chili powder
¼	cup fresh cilantro, chopped
12	(8- to 9-inch) flour tortillas
4–5	teaspoons canola or olive oil

1. Heat the oil in a large skillet over medium-high heat. Add the kale and sauté, stirring constantly, for 2 minutes, or until the kale starts to reduce. Add the corn and continue to sauté another 2 to 3 minutes, until the kale is tender and the corn is cooked.

2. In a large bowl, combine the cheese, black beans, chiles, cumin, chili powder and cilantro with the kale and corn. Mix gently to evenly distribute the kale.

3. Wipe out the skillet, heat on medium heat, and add about 1 teaspoon of canola oil to coat. Place a tortilla in the skillet. Put about ¾ cup of the cheese mixture in middle of the tortilla. Place another tortilla on top. When the tortilla is lightly golden, flip over. The quesadilla is done when the cheese is melted, 3 to 4 minutes. Repeat for the other quesadillas. Cut into wedges and serve.

Kale, Pumpkin Seed and Bacon Brittle

Everyone loves to munch on this brittle—bacon fans will love this combo. The original brittle recipe came from cookbook author and friend Kathy Gunst in her recent book of essays and recipes, *Notes from a Maine Kitchen*. I had tried Kathy's winning combination and told her I was going to try adding kale to it. She approved of the idea. She says the brittle will keep for several days in a cookie tin or resealable plastic bag—if it lasts that long.

3	strips bacon
1	cup pumpkin seeds
3	cups kale (stripped from stalk, chopped into bite-size pieces, rinsed and dried well)
1	cup sugar
	Pinch of salt
1½	tablespoons fresh rosemary, chopped
¼–½	teaspoon cayenne pepper
1	large egg white

1. Preheat the oven to 325°F.

2. To cook the bacon, heat a large skillet over medium-high heat and cook until crisp, being careful not to let it burn. Drain on a paper towel. Crumble into small, but not tiny, pieces and set aside.

3. Line a baking sheet with parchment paper, a silicon mat or aluminum foil.

4. In a medium-size bowl, mix the pumpkin seeds, kale, sugar, salt, rosemary, cayenne and bacon pieces.

5. In another bowl, whisk the egg white for a few minutes until foamy, but not stiff. Combine the egg white with the kale mixture—mix well with your hands to fully coat the kale.

6. Place the brittle mixture onto the prepared baking sheet, spreading it evenly with a soft spatula.

7. Bake for about 25 minutes, or until the brittle is a good golden brown color. Remove from the oven and let cool.

8. Break the brittle into 1½-inch pieces.

Potato Kale Latkes

Potatoes and kale have a natural affinity; the kale adds a character and flavor to regular potato latkes. Read the recipe through before starting so you understand about using the starch from the water the potatoes soak in; it keeps these potato pancakes from absorbing oil so they can stay crispy. These can also be served for dinner with beef, chicken or fish, and/or at breakfast or brunch with anything. Any leftovers reheat nicely the next day, in a skillet with a smidgeon of melted butter.

- 3 cups kale (stripped from stalk, finely chopped, rinsed and dried)
- 2 teaspoons olive oil
- Salt
- 2 pounds Idaho potatoes, peeled
- ½ cup finely minced onion (about ½ onion)
- ¼ cup all-purpose flour
- 2 large eggs
- Olive oil, peanut oil or butter, for cooking

DILL SOUR CREAM

- ½ cup sour cream or yogurt
- 1 tablespoon chopped fresh dill
- 2 teaspoons prepared horseradish (optional)
- Salt and freshly ground black pepper

1. Place the kale in a large bowl and add the 2 teaspoons olive oil and two pinches of salt. Massage the kale for 2 to 3 minutes. If it seems moist, use a few paper towels to absorb any excess moisture.

2. Either grate the potatoes with a box grater, or quarter them lengthwise and use the shredder attachment on a food processor. You should have about 6 cups. Place the grated potatoes in a bowl of water for 10 minutes or so. Line a second bowl with a clean kitchen towel or two layers of paper towels. Lift the potatoes out of the water a handful at a time, squeezing out the water with your hands over the soaking bowl as you go, and place in the clean towel or paper towels. Save the bowl with the soaking water and potato starch, and let the starch settle to the bottom (this might take a few minutes). Squeeze the towel to soak up any excess moisture from potatoes, getting them as dry as possible. Add the potatoes to the kale, along with the onion.

3. Pour off the water in the soaking bowl, leaving the starch at the bottom of the bowl (there will be up to 4 tablespoons). Add the eggs and flour to the starch and mix with a fork. Add this mixture to the latkes. Season with salt. (Sometimes I cook a test latke to help find the right level of salt.)

4. Heat one or two large skillets (nonstick work nicely) over medium-high heat and coat the bottom with about a tablespoon of olive oil or a combination of olive oil and a little butter. Pack a ¼-cup measuring cup with the potato mixture. Unmold into the skillet and place another few scoops of the mixture in the pan, without crowding, gently flattening each with a spatula. Panfry until each latke is golden, then gently flip and cook the other side, 10 to 14

minutes in total. Repeat with the remaining latke mixture. Place the latkes on a paper towel–lined baking sheet in a 200°F oven to keep warm, until ready to serve.

5. Serve with sour cream mixed with the chopped dill and horseradish, with salt and pepper to taste.

Cook's Note: When the times comes that I'm no longer testing kale recipes every day, I want to try these with half Idahos, half sweet potatoes, and also with a combination of shredded potato, carrot and parsnip or beet. We used to make these in cooking school and I have a feeling they'd work beautifully with kale.

Cocktails

Emerald Gimlet

Juice a few kale leaves in a juicer and store in the fridge until ready for your cocktails. You need a fine strainer to remove the grated ginger for a smooth, chilled emerald green gimlet.

- 2 ounces gin or vodka
- ½ ounce fresh kale juice
- ½ to 1 teaspoon grated fresh ginger
- ¾ ounce fresh lime juice
- ¾ ounce simple syrup (see cook's note)
- Lime wheel or small kale leaf, for garnish

In a mixing glass or shaker, combine the gin, kale juice, ginger, lime juice and syrup. Fill halfway with ice and shake vigorously for about 20 seconds, until very well chilled. Double strain into a martini or coupe glass through a small fine-mesh strainer, to catch the fresh ginger. Garnish with a lime wheel/and or a small piece of kale.

Cook's Note: To make simple syrup, add 1 cup of sugar to 1 cup of boiling water and stir until dissolved. Store in a mason jar; it keeps for weeks.

Kale Margarita

Save some of that juiced kale from the morning to make margaritas for your friends at night. Shaken over ice with fresh lime and orange liqueur, it's quite cooling (and quite green). This stellar idea came from Eva Sargent, the Southwest program director for Defenders of Wildlife, who makes margaritas with kale from her garden in Tucson, Arizona. I've altered it a bit since she makes it using Bacanora, a tequila-like liquor from agave roasted over pine fires, as well as an herbal liqueur from Mexico called Damiana. But that sure sounds good.

- 1½ ounces tequila
- ¾ ounce Patrón Citronge or Cointreau orange liqueur
- 1 ounce simple syrup (see cook's note)
- 1 ounce fresh lime juice
- ½ ounce fresh kale juice
- 2 drops orange bitters (optional, but nice)
- Lime wheel, for garnish

1. Place the tequila, liqueur, syrup, lime juice and kale juice in a shaker with ice. Shake well.
2. Pour over ice. Add the bitters, if using. Garnish with a lime wheel.

Booze Époque's Greener Pastures

Booze Époque is a boutique bartending catering company in Somerville, Massachusetts, owned by Meaghan Sinclair and Harmony Dawn. They create whimsical (and amazing) cocktails, using fresh, local, organic and seasonal ingredients, for private parties and special events. I gave them the challenge of creating a kale cocktail for this book, and they did not disappoint, especially in the whimsical and fun column. It does require a whipped cream dispenser to make kale foam that tops the drink, but hopefully you have one or can borrow one from a friend because you'll want to try this one.

COCKTAIL

- 2 slices of cucumber
- 5 mint leaves
- 1½ ounces Berkshire Mountain Greylock Gin
- ¼ ounce Dolin dry vermouth
- ¼ ounce fresh kale juice
- ¼ ounce fresh lime juice
- ¼ ounce simple syrup (see cook's note)
- ⅛ ounce green Chartreuse
- Small kale leaf, for garnish

FOAM

- ¼ ounce soy lecithin powder
- 2½ ounces fresh lemon juice
- 1¾ ounces fresh juiced kale
- ½ ounce simple syrup (see cook's note)
- Pinch of salt

1. To mix the cocktail: Muddle the cucumber and mint together in a shaker. Add the rest of ingredients, except the Chartreuse, and ice to the shaker. Shake. Double strain into a champagne coupe glass.

2. Foam: With a whisk, mix the soy lecithin with the lemon juice until the lecithin is dissolved. Place, along with the kale juice and syrup, in a whipped cream dispenser. Shake vigorously. Add roughly an inch of foam to the top of the cocktail.

3. Float the Chartreuse on top and add a kale leaf, for garnish.

Cook's Note: To make simple syrup, add 1 cup of sugar to 1 cup of boiling water and stir until dissolved. Store in a mason jar; keeps for weeks.

THE KALE CHRONICLES

Kale and Cocktails

I was supposed to be writing a book on homegrown cocktails, but somehow I ended up with a cookbook on kale instead. It started with a magazine piece I wrote on the very creative cocktails bartenders have been mixing up around the country—sometimes referred to as the garden-to-glass movement or craft cocktails. At some point in years past, I, like others, had abandoned cocktails in favor of wine or beer. But after taste-testing the new drink recipes, including a gin and tonic updated with grapefruit, cucumber, lime and St. Germain, I was smitten.

These new craft cocktails brimmed with new flavors and freshness. My newfound interest bordered on obsession. I began spending my creative energy making both cocktails and nonalcoholic drinks featuring fruits, vegetables, herbs and other vibrant ingredients. I worked on syrups with such flavors as lemongrass, ginger and vanilla. Friends and others who sampled wanted more. My husband's niece asked me to create a signature cocktail for her

wedding. Other friends started asking me to make specialty drinks, instead of food, at parties.

Why not elevate this new hobby to work, I wondered. I put together a proposal for homegrown drinks, as part of the process for getting a cookbook published. Claire, my agent, sent the drink proposal around to publishers, looking for one (or more) that might be interested.

One publisher, The Countryman Press of Vermont, upon seeing my previous books on greens and salads, made a counterproposal, asking asked whether I would be interested writing a book on kale.

A whole book on kale. Intriguing. I had already written a chapter on kale as part of my first cookbook, *Greens, Glorious Greens*. I had been eating kale and developing recipes for it since then, and had even organized the island's first Kale Festival with a local farmer. Although kale had become popular, I still witnessed people passing it by, trading their kale for something else at my local CSA. I figured maybe I could make a contribution to the field.

I laughed to myself. I guess the universe was saying maybe I should be spending my days eating healthy kale, not crafting cocktails and drinking.

When I started the kale book, I had not considered including a kale cocktail chapter. I hadn't even tried a kale cocktail or been anywhere that offered one. I wasn't sure I'd even enjoy one—until I tried one.

My first kale cocktail was made by Vineyard art gallery owner and cocktail crafting hobbyist Chris Morse. It was a version of a Bloody Mary he dubbed the Kale Mary. Chris pureed kale with a Bloody Mary mix and a touch of wasabi in the blender, garnishing the drink with a red hot pepper and a kale leaf. He had sent it along with his wife, Sheila, to our girls' night kale-testing party. We voted it the most creative dish made that night.

A few weeks later, Megan Ottens-Sargent, another gallery owner on Martha's Vineyard, told me about an Arizona friend who raved about kale margaritas, using kale from her garden. We sent for the recipe, and planned a testing night. The margarita called for one-third tequila, one-third kale juice and one-third Damiana or another liqueur, such as Grand Marnier, with a good squeeze of lime juice. I invited a few friends to join us for "kale cocktails."

Before the evening, I did a little research on the web and found quite a number of bartenders across the country also experimenting with kale and other greens. Given the kale craze, I shouldn't have been too surprised.

I started thinking of combinations I had used in the kale smoothies or juices that might also work for mixed drinks, such as pineapple and kale, or cucumber or celery with kale. I jotted down a few other ideas and prepped for experimentation: I juiced the kale, along with some limes and lemons and oranges, and made a ginger simple syrup.

The kale margarita was a hit. Next, we sampled a pineapple jalapeño margarita and thought that had potential as well. A kale lemon drop was also in the mix, using the ginger syrup and St. Germain liqueur, along with vodka, kale and fresh lemon juice. One test that sounded good on paper—vodka, cucumber, mint, kale and citrus— tasted just a tad bit too healthy.

The kale gimlet came along a few weeks later when Nicole Cabot, a friend and private chef, was sampling dishes after my regular Friday photo shoot. I had some kale juice, but she said she was not a fan of tequila.

"How about a gimlet?" she asked.

We mixed up kale juice, lime juice, ginger syrup and gin and shook it with ice. It tasted even better with freshly grated ginger. We sat around sampling a kale coleslaw and the final version of a Japanese noodle and kale soup, sipping our gimlet appreciatively. Nicole named it the Emerald Gimlet. Perfect.

Now that the book would include a kale cocktails chapter, I contacted my friends at Booze Époque in Somerville, Massachusetts. Meaghan and her partner, Harmony, describe their boutique catering bartending business as creating and serving whimsical cocktails using fresh, local and seasonal ingredients. I had a feeling they would be up for a kale cocktail challenge. No problem. After the holidays, I got an e-mail with two recipes. Their Kale Mary combined fresh tomatillos, serrano pepper and horseradish with kale. The Greener Pastures was even more fun: a gin drink topped with an inch of kale foam made in a whipped cream dispenser and drizzled with a bit of green Chartreuse, an herbal liqueur.

It's funny how things happen sometimes.

Kale Lemon Drop

Green and good!

6 pieces of fresh pineapple

1½ ounces vodka

¾ ounce fresh kale juice

¾ ounce fresh lemon juice

½ ounce simple syrup (see cook's note)

½ ounce St. Germain liqueur

½ egg white (optional)

1 piece of fresh pineapple or lemon wheel, for garnish

In a mixing glass or shaker, combine the pineapple, vodka, kale juice, lemon juice, simple syrup and St. Germain. With a muddler, crush the pineapple. Fill the mixing glass halfway with ice and add the egg white, if using. It gives the drink body and a bit of foam on top. Shake very well—at least 20 seconds. Strain into a martini or coupe glass. Garnish with a piece of pineapple or lemon wheel.

Cook's Note: To make simple syrup, add 1 cup of sugar to 1 cup of boiling water and stir until dissolved. Store in a mason jar; keeps for weeks.

Kale Mary

The duo at Booze Époque, a bartending catering company in Somerville, Massachusetts, created this Bloody Mary using kale and tomatillos, with a bit of heat from fresh horseradish and serrano peppers. A delicious addition to your brunch menu.

3 ounces tomatillo juice (from 3 to 4 tomatillos)

¼ ounce celery juice (from about ½ celery stalk)

⅛ ounce kale juice (from about 2 kale leaves)

1 slice of serrano pepper

⅛ teaspoon grated horseradish

1½ ounces blanco tequila

Pinch of salt

Pinch of freshly ground black pepper

¼ ounce Vida mezcal

Garnishes: 1 slice of tomatillo, wasabi microgreen, and/or a ring of sliced serrano

In a juicer, juice the tomatillos, celery and kale separately. In a cocktail shaker, muddle the serrano pepper; add the horseradish, tequila and the tomatillo, celery and kale juice; add the salt and pepper. Shake over ice. Double strain into a martini glass. Add a mezcal float. Garnish the side of the glass with a tomatillo round, wasabi microgreen, and/or a serrano slice.

Grains, Beans, Pasta and Pizza

Penne with Kale, Sausage and Mushrooms

This dish comes from White House chef and presidential valet Quincy Jackson, a fan of kale. I met Chef Quincy while he was on Martha's Vineyard, cooking for the First Family while they vacationed here in 2013.

- ½ pound penne pasta, preferably whole wheat
- 3 cups Italian (dinosaur) kale (stripped from stalk, cut in wide chiffonade and rinsed)
- 2 tablespoons olive oil
- ½ cup thinly sliced onion
- 2 garlic cloves, minced
- ½ pound spiced or mild Italian sausage, removed from casing
- 1 cup mushrooms, sliced (optional)
- 2–3 pinches of red pepper flakes
- 1 cup canned tomatoes, diced, or seeded and diced fresh tomatoes
- ¼ cup tomato paste
- 1¼ cups beef stock
- Salt
- 2 tablespoons fresh parsley, minced
- ¼ cup freshly grated Parmesan cheese

1. Bring a large pot of salted water to a boil and cook the pasta al dente, according to the package directions. About 4 minutes before the pasta is done, add the kale. Drain, and shake a few times to release the steam. Set aside.

2. In a large pan or skillet, heat the olive oil and sauté the onion for a few minutes. Add the garlic, sausage, mushrooms, if using, and a pinch or two of red pepper flakes, and quickly sauté, before adding the tomatoes, tomato paste and beef stock. Simmer for about 15 minutes. Season to taste with salt.

3. Mix in the pasta with the sauce. Garnish with the parsley and Parmesan.

Baked Stuffed Shells with Kale

In the New England area, there is a good-quality fresh mozzarella called Maplebrook, which is what I typically buy. Use your own favorite. Likewise, I've included a quick sauce recipe, but feel free to use your own or a favorite brand. Any type of kale will work here, though the Italian lacinato or Red Russian kale tends to cook down more like spinach, so I will use one of those if available. I cook the kale leaves whole first in the same water I will use to boil the pasta, and then chop them.

TOMATO SAUCE

2 (28-ounce) cans whole tomatoes	Good pinch of sugar
1 tablespoon olive oil	Salt
3 garlic cloves, finely minced	1 tablespoon chopped fresh parsley
1 teaspoon dried oregano	1 tablespoon chopped fresh basil

STUFFED SHELLS

4 cups whole kale leaves (stripped from stalk and rinsed)	½ cup Parmigiano-Reggiano cheese
1 (12-ounce) package jumbo shells pasta	1 large egg
Olive oil	¼ cup chopped fresh chives or scallions (or a bit of fresh basil, too)
2 cups ricotta cheese (16 ounces)	½ teaspoon kosher salt, or more to taste
1½ cups mozzarella cheese, cut into ¼-inch dice	¼ teaspoon freshly ground black pepper

1. Make the tomato sauce: Drain the juices and chop the tomatoes or pulse in a food processor to chop. Heat the olive oil, and sauté the garlic on low heat for 30 to 60 seconds. Add the tomatoes, oregano, sugar and salt to taste and bring to a boil. Turn down the heat and simmer, uncovered, for 10 minutes. Add most of the parsley (save some to garnish the shells) and basil and set aside to cool. Taste, and add additional sugar or salt to taste.

2. Make the stuffed shells: Bring a large pot of salted water to a boil. First, cook the kale for 4 to 5 minutes, until tender. Lift out the kale, drain and set aside. In the same pot of water after the kale is removed, cook the shells according to the package directions. Drain, shake to release the steam and drizzle the shells with olive oil to keep them from sticking. Set aside.

3. In a bowl, combine the cheeses, egg, chives, salt and pepper. Set aside.

4. After the kale has cooled, squeeze out any excess water. Chop into small pieces, and break apart a little as it tends to clump together when squeezed. You should have roughly 2 cups of cooked kale. Add to the cheese mixture, and stir until distributed.

5. To assemble: Ladle a thin layer of sauce on the bottom of a glass lasagne pan. With the spoon, stuff the shell with just enough filling so it still closes, then place seam side up into the baking pan, in rows. Repeat until the filling is used up. Ladle some of the sauce on top (you may have some leftover sauce). Sprinkle with additional parsley and Parmesan. Cover tightly with foil and bake for 35 to 40 minutes, until hot and bubbly.

Kale Pesto and Pasta

SERVES 4 TO 6

Here's another use for your garden kale—a quick pesto. Pine nuts are pricey these days, so this pesto uses walnuts instead, along with garlic, olive oil and Parmesan—flavors kale loves and ones that make pasta enjoyable. You can vary the pesto by adding fresh basil or parsley—see the cook's note. After blanching the kale, save its cooking water in the pot to boil the pasta in afterward.

5 cups kale leaves (stripped from stalk and rinsed)
2 large garlic cloves
½ cup walnuts, toasted
¼ cup Parmigiano-Reggiano cheese
⅓ cup olive oil
   Salt
1 pound pasta (spaghetti or desired shape)

1. Bring a pot of water to a boil and cook the kale in the boiling water for about 3 minutes. Lift out the kale leaves, drain and run under cold water to stop the cooking. Squeeze the kale to remove any excess water. Set aside, reserving the cooking water for the pasta.

2. Place the garlic in a food processor and chop. Add the kale and walnuts and pulse to chop. Add the cheese, olive oil and two pinches of salt. Process until combined, leaving a bit of texture.

3. Add salt to the cooking water, bring back to a boil and cook the pasta according to the package directions. Drain and place in a serving bowl. Immediately add a dollop of the kale pesto. Mix well. Refrigerate the remaining pesto.

Variations: The kale pesto gets a flavor boost with 1 cup of fresh basil leaves. Add to the food processor with the kale. Uses for the kale pesto include grain salads, other pasta dishes topped with chicken or vegetables, and vegetable soups.

Farro Kale Salad

I have always admired and appreciated the work of Martha's Vineyard photographer Randi Baird, whose crisp, colorful food photos have accompanied my work in numerous magazine articles. She lives in a cohousing community whose envious community garden—with its abundant kale and other vegetables—led to this amazing grain and green salad. It makes a great side with grilled chicken, beef or fish, or as part of a Greek or Middle Eastern feast.

5–6   cups kale (1 small bunch, stripped from stalk, torn or chopped into small pieces, rinsed and dried)
    Salt
1   tablespoon olive oil
1   cup farro, rinsed
½   small red onion, minced (about ½ cup)

3   tablespoons fresh dill, chopped
½   cup fresh parsley leaves, finely chopped
½   cup pomegranate seeds, 1 tart red apple, diced, or ½ cup dried cherries or cranberries (or any combination)
4   ounces feta cheese (½ cup)

DRESSING

2   tablespoons fresh lemon juice
3   tablespoons olive oil

Salt and freshly ground black pepper

1. Place the kale in a large bowl, salt lightly, and drizzle with the olive oil. Vigorously toss and massage the salt and oil into the kale until well coated. (Chop the kale additionally, if needed, after massaging.)

2. Place the farro in a large saucepan and cover with 2 quarts of salted water. Bring to a boil, lower the heat and simmer, uncovered, for 25 to 30 minutes. Drain well, and combine with the kale. Let cool completely, stirring occasionally.

3. Add the onion, dill and parsley to the kale mixture, along with the pomegranate seeds.

4. Make the dressing: Combine the lemon juice, olive oil, salt and pepper. Pour over the salad and gently toss. Place in a serving bowl or platter and top with the feta cheese.

Cook's Note: Farro is similar to barley when cooked, and has a nice toothy texture.

THE KALE CHRONICLES

A Love Affair with Kale and Feta

I have to apologize for my overuse of feta cheese.

Overuse of an ingredient has happened in my other books. In the soup book, it was leeks. At one point I realized that I used leeks in nearly every soup. Leeks add another level of flavor beyond onions. But did nearly every soup need one? The very first soup I made in high school was potato leek, and I still love that combination today and have made countless variations, including the cream of kale soup in this book. Farro was another discovery. I thoroughly enjoy the toothiness of farro instead of barley and created chicken farro soup, a beef and farro soup and even a kale farro soup. All delicious. But I had to force myself to stop—what if readers don't like farro, or can't locate it in their grocery store?

In some ways, cookbooks often reflect the likes and dislikes of the author. I noticed a whole chapter devoted to eggplant in Yotam Ottolenghi's book *Plenty*, a cookbook I enjoy cooking from. But I haven't tried one of the recipes, because I'm not an eggplant fan. And this is the price one can pay—everyone has different tastes. You might find one eggplant recipe in all four of my books. I don't love green peppers, either, and rarely use them.

About three months into writing *Kale, Glorious Kale*, I searched for the word *feta* in my manuscript to find a specific recipe, and realized it was happening again. *Feta* came up at least seven times. It made me a little sad because I was only halfway into testing recipes—what if feta was perfect for another recipe?

Let's see, I had a three dinner salads with baby kale and various vegetables, and some with fish or chicken. All had feta. The breakfast casserole combined eggs, kale, onions and feta. Oh, there were two egg and kale dishes with feta. Of course, I would add feta to the Greek greens dish spanakopita, now kale-kopita. And delicious, I might add.

It turns out that kale and feta taste great together. The slight saltiness and wonderful flavor of feta elevate kale, which needs salt and boosting complementary flavors. If you are ever wondering what cheese to use in a kale side dish or especially a salad, think no further.

As an aside, here's a word or two about feta in general. Not all types are created equal. I think that's the case with many foods. Some feta can be too salty. Some have little flavor. Feta can be different whether it's made from cow's milk, goat's milk or sheep's milk. And textures can vary.

Those made with sheep's milk are favorites, especially those made in France—including a Valbreso feta, and in Greece, among other European countries. The Greek often combine sheep's and goat's milk for some wonderful feta. I don't always love goat's milk alone—like goat cheese, it can taste too strong.

I did see a Bulgarian feta in bulk in the local supermarket one day, and thought I could save some money in my testing. It was too strong, and changed the whole flavor of the dish.

I had to laugh that two guest recipes in this book also have, you guessed it, feta. One is a kale salad that won the local kale fest. And to be fair, she's a cheese maker, and had made the feta cheese. The other is a great combination of kale, farro, apple, dill and feta.

Other cheeses do go well with kale, for the same reason feta works: the slight saltiness, the richness and overall flavor it brings to the earthy kale flavor. Parmesan cheese and kale taste delicious—on salads and in kale pesto. In fact, kale has an affinity to many cheeses including blue cheese, goat cheese and Cheddar. A friend who was recently living in Switzerland suggested Gruyère, and used it on her potato leek soup. I tried it with the kale soup with potatoes and leeks, and understood her choice. And now, whenever I can after I notice my fixation with feta and kale, I actively think: Can this work with another cheese?

While I'm at it, I should also apologize for probably having too much fruit in the book. I love all fruit. And I can't help it that fruit also tastes delicious with kale. Kale benefits from a touch of sweetness, especially in salads and smoothies. A few raisins, a juicy peach, apples, grapefruit, oranges, pineapple, mango, blueberries, dates, figs, plums, grapes and so on. There's a great spring salad using a simple combination of baby kale, fresh strawberries and feta . . . I mean goat cheese.

Fried Rice with Greens

It's true: Using cold, leftover rice seems to work best for making fried rice. If you can, make the rice the day before and store overnight in the fridge. Prep the vegetables before you start stir-frying, and this healthy dish cooks very quickly. I like combining the kale with Asian napa cabbage, if available, not only for the lighter contrast; its water content helps the kale soften as it cooks. The fish sauce adds another depth of flavor and blends right in. For vegetarians, substitute a bit of hot sauce. Eat the fried rice for dinner with a soup, bring to lunch or even enjoy for breakfast. The dish reheats nicely.

1 cup short-grain brown rice (about 3½ cups cooked)	1 cup shredded carrot (1 to 2 carrots)
Salt	1 cup corn kernels (stripped from 1 ear corn)
2 tablespoons coconut, canola or peanut oil, divided	2 teaspoons peeled and grated fresh ginger
	2 garlic cloves, finely minced
2 cups kale (stripped from stalk, chopped into small bite-size pieces and rinsed)	3 eggs, lightly beaten, or 1 cup diced extra-firm tofu
	2 tablespoons soy sauce
2 cups napa cabbage, thinly sliced into bite-size pieces (about ½ head)	1 tablespoon Asian fish sauce

1. Make the rice the day before: Rinse the rice and place in a saucepan with 2 cups of water and two pinches of salt. Bring to a boil, lower the heat and simmer on low, covered, for 38 to 40 minutes, until the water is absorbed. Do not stir or disturb while it cooks. When the rice is cooked, remove from the stove and let sit for 5 minutes. Place in a bowl and refrigerate overnight after stirring a couple of times to release the steam. (To make on the same day, let the rice cool on a baking sheet until the steam is released and then refrigerate while you are chopping the vegetables.)

2. When you are ready to fry the rice, place 1 tablespoon of your oil of choice in a wok or your largest heavy skillet. Add the kale and napa cabbage and cook on medium-high heat, stirring constantly (I use tongs or two wooden spoons) for 2 minutes. Add the carrot, corn, ginger and garlic and stir-fry for another 2 to 3 minutes. Transfer the vegetables to a bowl. Add 2 additional teaspoons of oil to the same pan and scramble the eggs. (Alternatively, you can scramble the eggs in a separate nonstick pan.) Add the cold cooked rice, soy sauce and fish sauce and mix well. Add the vegetables and stir until everything is hot. Serve immediately, and enjoy.

Cook's Notes:
- For more protein, add ½ (16-ounce) tub of tofu instead of the egg, or along with the egg. Cut the tofu into small cubes, less than ½ inch, and cook in a nonstick skillet with a film of oil until lightly golden, turning gently as you go.
- Sometimes fresh corn is unavailable; I've been told Cascadian Farms brand frozen corn still retains a bit of crunch. Or substitute fresh red bell pepper, diced tiny, and cook with the carrot.

Veggie Burgers with Kale

Nicole Cabot scored a bull's eye when she created these gluten-free veggie burgers. The burgers have a bit of everything—brown rice, beans, vegetables and kale—with just the right amount of flavor, yet they are still simple to make. Nicole, a private chef here on Martha's Vineyard, likes to serve these crispy burgers on a bed of greens with kimchi mayo. Alternatively, serve the burgers with a bun, lettuce, sliced tomato with Sriracha mayo, or without buns, topped with a tomato salsa.

1 cup short-grain brown rice (about 3½ cups cooked)

Salt

3 large kale leaves, stripped from stalk, chopped into small bits about ¼ inch and rinsed (about 2 cups)

2 teaspoons olive oil

½ cup finely grated carrot (smallest grate on a box grater)

¼ red bell pepper, seeded and finely diced

1 scallion, white and green parts, finely diced

1 (14-ounce) can chickpeas, or pinto or cannellini beans, drained and rinsed

2 teaspoons soy sauce

2 tablespoons ketchup

1 tablespoon grainy or Dijon mustard

Dash of Sriracha or hot sauce

1 tablespoon olive, avocado or coconut oil, for sautéing

1. Cook the brown rice in a small saucepan with 2¼ cups of water and two pinches of salt. Bring to a boil, and then simmer on low heat, covered, for about 40 minutes, or until all the water is absorbed. Let cool.

2. Place the kale in a bowl, and add the olive oil and two pinches of salt. Massage for 1 to 2 minutes, until reduced a bit. If the kale feels moist, squeeze out the moisture with a paper towel. Add the carrot, pepper and scallion. Set aside.

3. Place the beans in a large mixing bowl. Add the soy sauce, ketchup, mustard and Sriracha. Mash together with a potato masher and stir until most of the beans are smashed. A few whole beans are fine. Add the cooled rice and the kale mixture and mix well. Add additional salt, if needed. Squeeze the rice mixture a bit with your hands to break down the rice slightly, to help hold the burgers together. Form into six or seven patties, making each burger patty by forming back and forth between your hands until you compact it slightly. Chill for 30 minutes on a sheet pan lined with parchment paper. Don't skip this step, which helps the burgers set.

4. Heat your oil of choice in a large sauté pan on medium heat. Add the burgers without crowding them and cook for about 3 minutes on each side, until crispy on the outside and hot inside. Serve immediately.

Quinoa and Kale Salad

This is like eating the rainbow. Makes a good dish for a brunch, luncheon or potluck.

½ cup quinoa, rinsed

Kosher salt

4 cups kale (stripped from stalk, chopped into bite-size pieces, rinsed and dried)

1 tablespoon olive oil

1 cup fresh blueberries

1 mango, diced (1 to 1½ cups) (for how to peel a mango, see page 46)

½ cup pomegranate seeds (from ½ pomegranate), or ¼ cup dried cranberries

1 cup diced cucumber, peeled, seeds removed and diced small (from about 1 cucumber)

½ cup shredded carrot (1 medium-size carrot, peeled)

3 tablespoons chopped fresh mint leaves

CITRUS DRESSING

½ teaspoon orange zest

2 tablespoons fresh lemon juice

3 tablespoons fresh orange juice (from ½ orange)

4 tablespoons olive oil

½ teaspoon kosher salt

1. Place the quinoa, ¼ teaspoon of salt and ¾ cup of water in a saucepan. Bring to a boil, then lower the heat to low, cover, and cook for 12 to 13 minutes, until the water is absorbed. Turn off the heat and let the quinoa sit for 5 minutes. Remove the cover and set aside to cool completely.

2. While the quinoa is cooking, place the kale in a bowl. Add the olive oil and two pinches of salt and, with your hands, massage the kale for 2 to 3 minutes, rubbing the oil and salt into all the pieces. The kale will reduce in volume, turn a dark green and soften.

3. In a large serving bowl, combine the cooled quinoa, kale, blueberries, mango, pomegranate seeds, cucumber, carrot and mint.

4. Make the dressing: In a small bowl, whisk together the orange zest, lemon juice, orange juice, olive oil and salt. When ready to serve, add to the quinoa mixture and toss gently to combine. If you dress only what you are eating that day, the salad will keep nicely for a few days.

Variation: This salad also tastes great and looks beautiful without the quinoa. Add a portion of the dressing to your desired taste.

Tomato and Kale Pizza

This is a basic, delicious tomato and cheese pizza with additional flavor from fresh basil, Parmesan cheese and kale. This kale is precooked, but you can also use uncooked, massaged kale that becomes a bit crunchy. So many toppings taste great with kale; see sidebar for more ideas.

- 3 cups kale, stripped from stalk, roughly chopped, rinsed and dried)
- 1 tablespoon olive oil
- 2 garlic cloves
  Salt
- 1 ball pizza dough (page 47)
  Cornmeal, for sprinkling
- ¾ cup easy pizza sauce (page 48)
- ¼ cup fresh basil, slivered
- ¼ cup Parmesan cheese
- 1 cup shredded mozzarella or sliced fresh mozzarella, or more as desired

1. Place the pizza stone in the oven and preheat to 450°F for 30 minutes.

2. Bring about 4 cups of water to a boil in a sauté pan with a lid and add the kale. Cover and cook over high heat, stirring occasionally until tender, 4 to 6 minutes. Strain in a colander, and shake several times to release the steam, to stop the cooking. Dry the same skillet and heat the olive oil over medium-low heat. Add the garlic and sauté for 1 to 2 minutes, stirring the whole time to prevent the garlic from burning. Turn off the heat, add the kale and season with salt to taste. You should have about 1 cup of the cooked kale mixture.

3. Stretch the pizza dough into a 12-inch round. Sprinkle a pizza peel with cornmeal and place the dough on it (or place on a pizza pan or cooking sheet, either lined with a piece of parchment paper or greased with olive oil). Spread the pizza sauce on the dough with the back of a spoon, leaving a ½-inch border. Distribute the fresh basil and Parmesan over the sauce. Top with the mozzarella and the cooked kale.

4. Slide the pizza onto the stone and bake for 10 to 12 minutes, until the edges of the crust are golden.

Jessica's Kale and Feta Pizza

Jessica Roddy's kale and feta pizza was one of the three winning dishes at the Slow Food–sponsored kale festival at Mermaid Farm, a much-loved Vineyard farm that grows kale and sells feta as well. Jessica, a lawyer and mother of two here on the island, and I have had many foraging and cooking adventures together—including organizing the kale fest with farm owners Caitlin Jones and Allen Healy.

- 1 ball pizza dough (page 47)
- ½ cup mozzarella cheese, grated
- 1 onion, caramelized (see cook's note)
- ½ cup feta, broken into small chunks
- 4 large kale leaves, stripped from stalk, torn into 1-inch pieces, rinsed and dried
  Olive oil

1. Preheat the oven to 450°F. Roll out the pizza dough until thin on a lightly floured board and transfer to a large, greased baking sheet. Top with the mozzarella, caramelized onion and feta and cover with the kale. Drizzle with olive oil.

2. Bake for 15 minutes.

Cook's Note: To caramelize an onion: Slice the onion thinly and sauté in 1 tablespoon of olive oil over very low heat, covered, stirring occasionally, until slightly browned and truly delicious. Add a little sea salt, if you like, while it is cooking.

3 PIZZA IDEAS

Portobello Mushroom, Roasted Red Pepper and Kale Pizza

- 1 ball pizza dough (page 47)
- 2 tablespoons olive oil
- 2 portobello mushrooms, stemmed, sliced and sautéed with 1 minced garlic clove
- Salt and freshly ground black pepper

- 1 small red pepper, roasted and sliced
- ¾ cup easy pizza sauce (page 48)
- 1 cup cooked kale
- 1–1½ cups shredded mozzarella cheese

Kale, Fig Spread, Caramelized Onion and Goat Cheese Pizza

- 1 ball pizza dough (page 47)
- 2 tablespoons roasted garlic
- ¼ cup fig spread or fresh figs
- ½ cup caramelized onion (see cook's note, facing page)
- 1 cup cooked kale
- ½ cup goat cheese
- 8–10 pitted kalamata olives

Sausage, Kale and Caramelized Onion Pizza

- 1 ball pizza dough (page 47)
- ¾ cup tomato sauce
- ½ cup caramelized onion (see cook's note, facing page)
- ½ cup cooked and crumbled sausage
- 1 cup shredded mozzarella
- 2 cups massaged kale (see page 30)

Chickpea and Kale Salad

After a quick massage of the raw kale, it's combined with classic Mediterranean flavors of feta, roasted pepper, lemon, garlic and olives. It's easy to double the recipe and bring it as a potluck dish. When doubling, I usually roast red and yellow bell peppers to make the salad even more colorful. It tastes best at room temperature, dressed just before serving.

1 red bell pepper	1 (15-ounce) can chickpeas, drained and rinsed
3 cups kale leaves, stripped from stalks, chopped into small bite-size pieces, rinsed and dried	¼ cup red onion, finely minced (about ¼ onion)
1 tablespoon olive oil	⅓ cup pitted kalamata olives, cut lengthwise into quarters
Salt	½ cup crumbled French or Greek feta cheese

LEMON DRESSING

2 tablespoons fresh lemon juice	⅛ teaspoon smoked sweet paprika or cayenne pepper
½ teaspoon finely minced garlic	
½ teaspoon dried oregano	3 tablespoons olive oil
¼ teaspoon ground cumin	¼ teaspoon salt
	Freshly ground black pepper

1. Place the red pepper over an open flame on the burner (or under the oven broiler if you have an electric stove). Use a pair of tongs to turn the pepper as it blackens on each side. Place in a paper bag or bowl with a plate on top to "steam" for 10 minutes. Remove the charred exterior under running water, removing the top and seeds as you go. Dry with a paper towel and cut into a medium dice.

2. Put the kale in a serving or salad bowl along with the olive oil and two pinches of salt. Massage the kale until glistening and tender, 2 minutes or so. If it seems moist, dab it with a paper towel. Add the chickpeas, red pepper, red onion and olives. Mix gently.

3. Make the dressing: Whisk together the lemon juice, garlic, oregano, cumin, paprika, olive oil, salt and black pepper.

4. Just before serving, add all the dressing to the salad, and gently toss. Crumble the feta cheese on top. Serve at room temperature.

Wheat Berry Salad with Pomegranate and Kale

Wheat berries—the kernels of unprocessed whole wheat sold in bulk bins or packages marked whole wheat or wheat berries—make an especially wonderful grain salad, especially colorful and nutritious tossed with pomegranate seeds and chopped baby kale. This is a salad for anytime, but the red and green look great for Thanksgiving or holiday season. This would go nicely with fish for dinner as well.

1 cup wheat berries

Salt

1 cup pomegranate seeds (from about 1 pomegranate) (see page 46 for how to open a pomegranate)

⅓ cup dried cranberries, roughly chopped

2 cups baby kale (stemmed, sliced, rinsed and dried) (see cook's note)

1 cup sliced almonds or walnuts, lightly toasted

RASPBERRY DRESSING

⅓ cup fresh or frozen raspberries

3 tablespoons fresh orange juice (from ½ orange)

3 tablespoons olive oil

1 teaspoon pure maple syrup or honey

1 tablespoon fresh lime juice or balsamic vinegar

½ teaspoon kosher salt

1. Rinse the wheat berries and place in a large saucepan filled with enough salted water to cover them by several inches. Bring to a boil, then lower the heat to a simmer, partially cover, and cook the wheat berries until they are plump and tender, about 1 hour 20 minutes. (Be sure to add 1 to 2 teaspoons of salt to the water to boost the flavor of the grain.) Test as you cook; cooked wheat berries are still somewhat chewy. Drain, and set aside to cool completely.

2. Combine the cooled wheat berries with the pomegranate seeds, cranberries and kale. A nice wide platter will show off the salad nicely.

3. Make the dressing: Combine the raspberries, orange juice, olive oil, maple syrup, lime juice, and salt in a food processor or blender. (If using frozen raspberries, let the mixture sit for a few minutes while the berries defrost.) Process or blend the dressing until smooth. When ready to serve, pour over the salad and toss. The wheat berries will absorb dressing, so dress the salad generously. Test after a few minutes to make sure it's just right. Top with the nuts and serve.

Cook's Note: If baby kale is unavailable, substitute raw massaged kale. Start with 4 cups of kale chopped into bite-size pieces. Massage for 2 to 3 minutes with 2 teaspoons of olive oil and two pinches of salt.

Asian Peanut Noodle and Kale Salad

Raw, kneaded kale and a few other colorful vegetables and edamame pair with noodles and a peanut sauce featuring ginger, lime and honey. Italian kale works best here because it can be cut into thin strips and reduces nicely, kneaded with a bit of sesame oil and salt. Serve alongside grilled steak, shrimp or chicken for dinner. Or add shredded cooked chicken or sliced steak right to the dish.

- 1 (8- to 9-ounce) package soba noodles (see cook's note)
- 5 teaspoons dark sesame or peanut oil, divided
- 4 cups kale (about ½ bunch, stripped from stalk, sliced thinly into ¼-inch strips, rinsed and dried)

- 2 good pinches of salt
- 1 cup shredded carrot (from 1 to 2 carrots)
- ½ cup thinly sliced radish (cut into thin half-moons)
- 1 cup frozen shelled edamame
- ⅓ cup unsalted peanuts, chopped

LIME AND PEANUT DRESSING

- 3 tablespoons peanut butter
- 2 tablespoons water
- 2 tablespoons fresh lime juice
- 2–3 teaspoons honey

- 1 tablespoon soy sauce
- 2 tablespoons peanut or vegetable oil
- 2 teaspoons grated fresh ginger
- ¼ teaspoon Sriracha or hot sauce, or more to taste

1. Cook the soba noodles in salted water according to the package directions. Aim for the lower cooking time because soba noodles can easily overcook. Drain, then continue to shake the strainer to release the steam and stop the cooking. Add 2 teaspoons of the sesame oil and shake again to distribute and keep the noodles from sticking. Set aside.

2. Place the kale in a large serving bowl or salad bowl and add the remaining 3 teaspoons of sesame oil and the salt. Massage for 2 to 3 minutes, working the oil into the kale leaves. Add the carrot and radish. Run hot water over the edamame for 30 seconds, drain and add.

3. Make the dressing: Whisk together the peanut butter, water, lime juice, honey, soy sauce, peanut oil, ginger and Sriracha in a bowl. Taste with a few of the noodles, and add additional soy sauce or salt, if needed.

4. Just before serving, mix the dressing with the noodles. Using tongs will help. Add to the kale mixture and mix again. Garnish with the chopped peanuts. Serve at room temperature.

Cook's Note: I typically use Eden Foods wheat and buckwheat soba noodles, but Eden udon noodles are a nice choice, too. I'm sure any favorite noodle would work fine.

Summer Pasta with No-Cook Kale and Tomatoes

A very easy summer dish with fresh juicy tomatoes, garlic and kale. The finishing touch is a topping of crispy bread crumbs and Parmesan. Use any kale here, but if you think it might be too tough to soften with a quick massage, you can always cook the kale in the last few minutes of cooking the pasta. Serve with a salad, maybe even a kale Caesar salad that shares some of the pasta ingredients.

3 cups kale (stripped from stalk, chopped into ¼-inch pieces, rinsed and dried)

3 tablespoons olive oil, divided

Salt

2 teaspoons finely minced garlic (use a garlic press if you have one)

2 teaspoons lemon zest

3 anchovy fillets, finely chopped (optional, but tasty)

1 cup chopped fresh tomatoes

12 ounces spaghetti pasta

TOPPING

⅓ cup panko bread crumbs

¼ cup Parmigiano-Reggiano cheese

2 teaspoons olive oil

1. Place the kale in a wide pasta bowl. Add 1 tablespoon of the olive oil and two pinches of salt. Massage the kale until it's glistening and reduced in size. Chop the kale additionally if any pieces are not minced.

2. Add the garlic to the kale, along with the lemon zest and anchovies. Mix in well and top with the tomatoes and a few pinches of salt.

3. In a small bowl, mix the panko, Parmigiano-Reggiano, and 2 teaspoons of the oil. Set aside for topping.

4. Bring a large pot of salted water to a boil, and cook the pasta according to the package directions. (Make sure there's plenty of salt in the water to flavor the pasta.) Save ½ cup of the pasta water. Drain the pasta, and quickly mix the hot pasta with the kale mixture, along with the reserved pasta water and remaining 2 tablespoons of oil. Stir well and top with the bread crumb mixture. Serve hot.

Wild Rice and Kale—Stuffed Butternut Squash

SERVES 2 (OR 4 AS A SIDE)

This delicious dish was created by Denise Woodward of Chez Us, a personal food website. It first appeared on the Eat Boutique site, a magazine and market that discovers and celebrates small-batch foods by boutique food makers. I usually double this recipe for company or simply to have leftovers.

- 1 (2½-pound) butternut squash, cut in half and seeded
- 5 tablespoons olive oil, divided, plus more for brushing squash
- Salt and freshly ground black pepper
- ¼ cup minced yellow onion
- ¼ cup minced celery
- ½ cup brown and wild rice mixture

- 1 cup vegetable stock or water
- 6 large cremini mushrooms, sliced
- 2 garlic cloves, finely minced
- 1 tablespoon fresh sage, finely chopped
- 2 teaspoons fresh thyme, chopped
- ½ bunch lacinato kale, stripped from stalk, thinly sliced and rinsed (3 to 4 cups)

1. Preheat the oven to 425°F.

2. Place the butternut squash on a baking sheet and brush with olive oil. Roast, cut side down, for about 20 minutes. Turn cut side up and continue to roast for another 15 to 20 minutes, or until the squash is tender, but not collapsed or overdone. Remove from the oven, sprinkle with salt and pepper and set aside.

3. Place 2 tablespoons of the olive oil in a medium-size saucepan and heat over medium heat. Add the onion and celery, stir and cook for 3 minutes. Add the rice and continue to cook until lightly browned and fragrant, stirring the entire time. Pour the stock into the rice mixture and bring to a boil. Simmer, covered, over low heat for 40 to 45 minutes, or according to the package instructions. Fluff with a fork.

4. In a large skillet, heat the remaining 3 tablespoons of oil over medium heat. Add the mushrooms and cook over low heat until golden brown, about 8 minutes. Stir in the garlic and herbs and cook for 1 minute. Add the kale and cook until wilted and cooked, 3 to 4 minutes. Remove from the heat.

5. Scoop out some of the butternut squash and cut into small pieces. Return the shell of the squash to the baking sheet.

6. Fold the rice and squash into the kale mixture, then gently fill each of the squash shells. Return to the oven and reheat for 10 minutes.

Kale, Onion and Sausage Calzones

Warm from the oven, a bite into these pizza packages tells you the combination of kale, sausage, onion and cheese works. James, my high schooler, said he could eat one of these every day of the week. These make good party food or a casual dinner accompanied by a soup or salad. They reheat well.

2   balls pizza dough (page 47)

1   bunch kale, stripped from stalk, chopped into bite-size pieces and rinsed (about 6 cups)

2   tablespoons olive oil

1   large onion, diced (about 2 cups)

3   garlic cloves, finely minced

¾   pound of your favorite sausage, removed from casing

Salt

1½   cups mozzarella cheese, grated (fresh mozzarella is nice)

1   cup fontina cheese, grated

2   cups tomato sauce (page 48)

1   egg, for egg wash

Cornmeal, for dusting

1.   Preheat the oven to 450°F. If you have a pizza stone, place it in the oven.

2.   In a skillet with a lid, bring 4 cups of water to a boil. Add the kale, cover, and cook on high heat for 4 to 5 minutes. Drain, and cool by shaking to release the steam. Set aside.

3.   Wipe the skillet dry. Heat the olive oil, add the onion and sauté for 8 to 10 minutes. Add the garlic and stir until sizzling, about 1 minute more. Add the sausage and cook until no longer pink, breaking it up as you cook. Use a paper towel to mop up any fat released from the sausage. Remove from the heat, and add the kale and a pinch or two of salt.

4.   Combine the two cheeses. Have a baking sheet ready, lined with parchment paper.

5.   Cut each pizza ball into four pieces and form each into a ball. Dust the counter with flour and roll out one of the mini balls to a disk 6 or 7 inches in diameter. Spoon on 2 tablespoons of the sauce, add about ½ cup of the kale filling and top with ¼ cup of the cheese mixture.

6.   Fold the pizza dough in half over the filling into the shape of a half-moon, and bring the edges together. Press the edges to seal. Roll the edge up once to form a lip (or you can press the edge with a fork). Place on the prepared baking sheet. Repeat the process until all the pizza balls are rolled out and filled. Whisk the egg in a small bowl and with a pastry brush, lightly coat the calzone with the egg wash—which gives the finished product a nicer look.

7.   Dust the pizza stone or a baking sheet with cornmeal. Add half of the calzones, if they fit, to the stone and bake for 10 to 12 minutes, until the crust is golden. (If using a baking sheet, you might be able to fit all the calzones.) Enjoy!

salads

Kale, Celery, Date and Apple Salad

This salad works best with the tender baby kale, now available at many farmers' markets and in supermarkets labeled as "baby kale"—usually in the clear plastic boxes. Use juicy orange slices instead of apples in the winter for a variation, or omit the apples when making in the spring or summer.

4 cups baby kale (stemmed, washed and dried)	1 lemon wedge
8 pitted dried dates (try to find soft, not dried-out dates)	½ cup walnuts, toasted and chopped
2 celery stalks	½ cup feta cheese, crumbled
1 crisp red apple (organic if possible, as it won't be peeled)	

BALSAMIC VINAIGRETTE

4 teaspoons balsamic vinegar	3 tablespoons olive oil
1 teaspoon pure maple syrup or other sweetener	Salt and freshly ground black pepper

1. Place the baby kale in a wide serving bowl or platter. Cut the dates, lengthwise, into very thin strips, and place in a small separate bowl. Peel the celery and cut in half lengthwise. With your knife at a diagonal angle, cut very thin, 1- to 2-inch pieces of celery. Add to the dates. Slice the sides off the apple and cut those pieces into very thin slices. Squeeze lemon juice over the apple slices, to keep them from browning.

2. Make the dressing: In a small bowl, whisk together the vinegar, maple syrup and olive oil. Season with two pinches of salt and a few grinds of pepper.

3. Just before serving, pour most of the dressing over the salad and toss to combine; pour the rest over the celery and dates. Top with the date mixture, apple slices, walnuts and feta cheese.

Cook's Note: Some feta cheese has little flavor, surprisingly. But the French sheep's milk feta is usually flavorful, as is the Greek feta that is a combination of sheep's and goat's milk.

Raw Kale Crunch Salad

Kale, broccoli *and* seaweed—this could be one of the most health-packed salads I've ever made, and that's saying a lot. It's also delicious, with a tangy lemon-sesame dressing, as well as colorfully appealing. Don't be intimidated by arame seaweed; it's very mild tasting and full of iron and calcium, as are the kale, broccoli and sesame seeds.

- 4 cups chopped kale (stripped from stalk, cut into bite-size pieces, rinsed and dried)
- 1 tablespoon olive oil
- 2 pinches of salt
- 2 cups broccoli florets, cut into tiny florets
- 1 large carrot, peeled and cut into matchsticks or shredded

- 2 cups red cabbage, sliced as thinly as you can
- 4 radishes, thinly sliced, then cut into half-moons (optional)
- ½ cup dried arame seaweed (optional)
- 2 tablespoons sesame seeds, toasted

TAHINI LEMON DRESSING

- 2 tablespoons fresh lemon juice
- 2 tablespoons tahini
- 2 teaspoons pure maple syrup
- ½ teaspoon fresh finely minced garlic (1 small clove)

- 4 tablespoons olive oil
- 2 teaspoons soy sauce, and/or salt to taste
- 1 tablespoon water
- Salt

1. Place the kale in a wide salad bowl. Sprinkle with the olive oil and salt. Massage with your hands for 2 to 3 minutes, until the kale is reduced and glistening. It should taste good. (If it seems moist, use a paper towel to blot up some of the moisture.) Mix in the broccoli, carrot, cabbage and radishes, if using.

2. Put the arame, if using, in a small bowl and cover with 1 cup of hot water to hydrate. After at least 5 minutes, drain, dry with a paper towel and make one or two cuts to cut the long strands just a bit. Add to the salad.

3. Make the dressing: Whisk together the lemon juice, tahini, maple syrup, garlic, olive oil, soy sauce, water and salt to taste in a small bowl. Add additional water if it's too thick. Try a bit of the salad in a small bowl with the dressing to see if you need to make any adjustments. Just before serving, dress the salad (you may not need all the dressing) and toss with tongs. Top with the sesame seeds.

Cook's Note: If tahini, a thick paste made from ground sesame seeds, is unavailable, add 2 additional tablespoons of olive oil to the dressing, and omit the water. Daikon radish can be substituted for regular pink radish. Daikon radish looks like a large white carrot. If using, peel, slice thinly, then cut the slices into matchsticks.

THE KALE CHRONICLES

Baby Kale: New to the Marketplace

One of my favorite aspects of being a food writer is discovering new foods or ingredients that become favorites. While researching and writing this book I fell in love with baby kale.

It did not exist as a concept or product when I wrote the kale chapter in *Greens, Glorious Greens* in 1996. It's interesting, neither did the ubiquitous kale chips or massaged kale salads. Had I included this kale trifecta in the earlier book, maybe I'd be a kale-loving millionaire by now.

Baby kale had to exist though, because it is simply the leaves picker earlier and smaller. Back then, no growers chose to market it as they are now. From seed to plant, in three weeks, a small kale leaf, two to three inches long, emerges. At this stage, it's as tender as a leaf of lettuce or arugula, and growers snip off large swatches with a sharp knife. Baby kale leaves lack the boldness or aftertaste of more mature kale. Still, baby kale retains a bit of the hardiness of the parents and holds up when dressed in a salad, avoiding deflation or sogginess.

It is, in short, perfect for salads, and has become my new favorite. (Sorry, my old friend arugula.) It doesn't require any special treatment; you simply wash it and spin dry.

Add spring strawberries and feta; or roasted pears, spiced nuts and blue cheese in the fall. My favorite summer kale combination is one juicy, flavorful peach with fresh mozzarella cheese. I marinate the mozzarella in the dressing, and after a bit, pour both over the peach slices and baby kale. The first time I made this and served it to my husband, he didn't miss a beat: "Are these the very expensive Goldbud peaches we're eating?" "Yes," I said softly, hoping to be inaudible.

This led to the series of dinner kale salads in the book. This is the answer to a meal you don't have to cook, but can feed fresh, healthy food in a snap to a gathering. I tried the first one with chunks of smoked salmon fillets, garden tomato and cucumber, feta cheese, hard-boiled eggs, rolled prosciutto and thinly sliced red onion. All were sectioned over baby kale. It fed seven easily. *A keeper recipe*, I noted in my head.

"That was kale?" my aunt asked, looking at the empty platter.

Next came baby kale smoothies. There is no end to uses for baby kale.

Susie Middleton, another cookbook author here on the Vineyard, wrote a blog called "New at the Grocery Store: Baby Kale and 10 Ways to Use It." It was one of her most popular blogs, she told me.

She recommends adding baby kale to eggs or frittata-like mixtures for breakfast, using it as a "topper" for pizza dough or grilled bread or a "filler" in a quesadilla or taco. She suggests making quick soups using baby kale and quick sautés, even combining fish with baby kale sautéed in olive oil with ginger, garlic and lemon zest. For her full list of ten, see http://sixburnersue.com.

Debby Farber of Blackwater Farm in West Tisbury, Massachusetts, one of my favorite growers here, introduced me to baby kale. She even bagged a few seeds for me to grow. I literally mixed up the soil a bit, threw on the seeds, and in three weeks my own patch was growing. This was late September in New England. I was still picking baby kale late into the fall, even brushing off the snow one December afternoon to find the bright, perky baby leaves underneath. She gave me Red Russian kale seeds, to grow the somewhat frilly green leaf with reddish-purple veins. Next year I also want to try the lacinato or Tuscan baby kale as well. You snip and it regrows, round after round. It was quite a savings when I was writing this book and testing the kale salads.

Almost immediately after, I began seeing baby kale packaged in plastic boxes in the supermarket. I noticed two growers at the Portland, Maine, farmers' market carrying bags of baby kale, and as well as a farmers' at another New England market. By the time this book hits shelves, I expect to see it everywhere. And you have a whole chapter of recipes to try it with.

The only drawback of baby kale may be pinching off the baby stems. I spent a few minutes doing this one night for our salad. I guessed I missed a few, according to my 14-year-old son, who said: "Nice salad, but I don't like the stems."

Chicken Salad with Kale, Oranges, Snap Peas & Red Pepper SERVES 6

Colorful vegetables look appealing next to the dark green kale and strips of roasted chicken. You can quickly roast split chicken breasts, grill boneless chicken or use rotisserie-cooked chicken, either shredded into larger pieces or diced. Regular kale can easily be replaced by baby kale, if available (use about 6 cups). This basic recipe of the kale and chicken can be turned into many variations; see cook's note.

3 bone-in split chicken breasts, or 3 cups cooked chicken

Olive oil

Salt

8 cups kale (about 1 bunch, stripped from stalk, chopped into bite-size pieces, rinsed and dried)

2 cups snap peas

1 red bell pepper, peeled, seeded and cut into thin strips

3 navel oranges, outside peel removed with a serrated knife, orange sliced into rounds, then cut into half-moons

1–2 tablespoons sesame seeds, toasted

CITRUS DRESSING

2 tablespoons fresh lime juice

2 tablespoons fresh orange juice

2 teaspoons honey

4 tablespoons peanut, canola or vegetable oil

1 teaspoon finely grated fresh ginger

1 teaspoon soy sauce

1. Preheat the oven to 350°F. Place the split chicken breasts on a rimmed cookie sheet lined with foil or parchment paper for easy cleanup. Rub both sides of the chicken with olive oil and sprinkle generously with salt. Roast for about 45 minutes, or slightly longer for very large pieces, or until the chicken registers 160° to 165°F on an instant-read thermometer. You can also check for doneness by making a small cut with a knife. Let the chicken cool to room temperature, then remove the skin and bones, and shred into bite-size strips along the grain.

2. Place the kale in a wide salad bowl. Sprinkle with 1 tablespoon of olive oil and two pinches of salt. Massage with your hands for 2 to 3 minutes, until the kale is reduced and glistening. It should taste good. (If it seems moist, use a paper towel to take out some of the moisture.)

3. Bring a small pot of water to a boil and parboil the snap peas for 30 seconds, until they turn bright green. Drain, and rinse with cold water to stop the cooking. Dry on a paper towel.

4. Make the dressing: Whisk together the lime juice, orange juice, honey, your oil of choice, ginger and soy sauce in a small bowl.

5. Place the kale on a large platter and pour half of the dressing over it. Mix well. In the empty kale bowl, combine the chicken, snap peas and red pepper and mix with the rest of the dressing and a pinch or two of salt. Add to the top of the kale. Add the orange segments. Sprinkle with sesame seeds.

Cook's Note: Using a template of massaged kale and cooked chicken, add grapes, apples and walnuts and a lemon dressing with a bit of mayonnaise. Try one with massaged kale, bacon, chicken, fresh tomatoes and croutons, with a kale pesto mixed with some mayonnaise.

Kale and Avocado Salad

This salad is dressed right in the bowl just before serving—making it very easy indeed. Use baby kale for this salad, or if unavailable, substitute regular kale that is massaged, see page 30. Surprisingly, lime juice is often just as nice for a salad as lemon juice. Give it a try.

6 cups baby kale (longer stems removed, rinsed and dried)
Olive oil
Salt

Fresh lime or lemon juice (from ½ lemon or lime)
1 just-ripe avocado, pitted and diced
Parmesan cheese

1. Place the baby kale leaves in a wide shallow serving dish or bowl. Add a drizzle of olive oil (enough to lightly coat the leaves), and with a pair of tongs, mix well. Add two pinches of salt and a light squeeze of lime juice. Mix again with the tongs. Taste a piece. It should taste good, with a hint of citrus and olive oil, lightly salted. Make any adjustments needed.

2. Add the avocado, squeeze a bit more citrus juice over the avocado and add a pinch of salt. Mix in well. Garnish with grated Parmesan to taste. Serve immediately.

Kale Revolution in a Bowl

I heard raves about this salad even before I had a chance to try it. It comes from Tamara Weiss, owner of Midnight Farm home goods and clothing on Martha's Vineyard, who says she always leaves with an empty bowl at the end of a party. She says any variety of kale, or a mix of varieties, will work with this salad, but her favorite is the Italian lacinato kale. She saves the kale stalks to sauté with ginger or stir-fry later.

1½ cups salted hazelnuts

5–6 bunches lacinato kale, or more for a large party, stripped from the stalk, torn or roughly chopped, rinsed and dried (about 16 cups)

⅓ cup goji berries (see cook's note)

DRESSING

1 cup fresh organic lemon juice (5 to 6 lemons)

1 medium-size to large whole head of garlic, chopped by hand or in a food processor

1 cup olive oil

Freshly ground black pepper

1 hunk of Parmesan cheese (slice of pie equivalent), grated coarsely, not finely

1. Toast the hazelnuts in a skillet until lightly browned, stirring occasionally, 5 to 8 minutes. Let cool. Roughly chop by hand or in a food processor.

2. Place the kale in a large bowl and massage with your hands until a darker green color and reduced in size, about 10 minutes. This can be done earlier in the day and stored in the fridge.

3. Make the dressing: Combine the lemon juice, garlic and olive oil in a quart-size jar. Season with pepper to taste. (There should be enough salt on salad from the salted hazelnuts.) Shake well. Add the Parmesan and shake again. The dressing should be thick and creamy.

4. To serve, place the massaged kale in your favorite wide serving bowl. Dress with your desired amount of dressing (you will have extra dressing). Mix well. Toss in the goji berries and chopped hazelnuts.

Cook's Note: Goji berries are bright, orange-red berries that come from a shrub native to China, where it has been eaten for generations in the hopes of living longer. Tamara recommends a brand of organic goji from Navitas Naturals. They add a beautiful color contrast to the kale, though you can substitute another dried fruit as well as mixing the nuts with walnuts or sesame seeds.

Kale-slaw

This looks very colorful, especially if you can combine red and green cabbage with the dark green kale and carrots. Use whatever type of kale softens best for you when massaged. I've used the curly kale a lot as well as lacinato or Tuscan kale; just do your best to slice thinly through the curls. Alternatively, you can use baby kale and slice that into slivers after removing the stems.

- 8 cups kale (about 1 bunch, stripped from stalk, sliced into slivers, rinsed and dried)
- 1 tablespoon olive oil
- ½ teaspoon kosher salt
- 2 cups red or green cabbage, or a combination, sliced as thinly as possible

- 1 cup grated carrot (about 2 medium-size carrots, peeled)
- 1 cup thinly sliced napa cabbage (optional)
- ½ cup toasted sunflower seeds

LEMON DRESSING

- 2 tablespoons fresh lemon juice
- 1 tablespoon finely minced shallots
- 1 teaspoon sugar

- 3 tablespoons mayonnaise
- 5 tablespoons olive oil
- Salt and freshly ground black pepper

1. To massage the kale, place the kale in a large serving platter or dish. Add the olive oil and salt and massage for 2 to 3 minutes, until the kale is soft and tender. Mix in the cabbage, carrot and napa cabbage, if using.

2. Make the dressing: In a small bowl, whisk together the lemon juice, shallots, sugar, mayonnaise, and olive oil. Season with salt and four to five grinds of pepper. Taste-test the dressing on a few spoons of the slaw; adjust the salt and pepper, if necessary. Just before serving, mix the dressing with the coleslaw. Top with the sunflower seeds.

Variations: For sweets lovers like myself, some raisins, dried cranberries or cherries are a nice addition.

Shredded Brussels Sprout and Kale Salad

Connie Warden, an artist and longtime chef/restaurant owner from Saint Albans, Vermont, thought that she might try to offset her bad habits by just eating kale every day. "I don't know for sure that the plan has worked, but after returning from two months in Oregon of wining and dining, I was so happy to see the kale still waving at me." She developed this cool salad combining kale with shredded Brussels sprouts, orange slices and dates and reports that it's good with grilled salmon, chicken thighs or grocery store rotisserie chicken on top—or even cooked beans. "Also, a good old hard-boiled or a nice soft-poached egg is magic." Connie was named Vermont Chef and Restaurateur of the Year in 2004.

4 cups kale, if tender (stripped from stalk, rinsed and dried), or baby kale, or 6 cups chopped kale to massage (see page 30)

2 cups shredded raw Brussels sprouts (halved and thinly sliced)

Big handful of arugula (if available)

1 orange, outside peel removed with a serrated knife, orange thinly sliced

½ cup chopped pitted dates

Handful of toasted pumpkin seeds

Crumbled feta cheese

POMEGRANATE VINAIGRETTE

1 tablespoon pomegranate molasses (see cook's note)

2 tablespoons fresh orange juice

2 tablespoons water

⅛ teaspoon smoked paprika

4 tablespoons olive oil

Salt and freshly ground black pepper

1. Toss together the kale, Brussels sprouts, arugula, if using, orange slices and dates.

2. Make the vinaigrette: Whisk together the pomegranate molasses, orange juice, water, paprika and olive oil. Season with salt and pepper.

3. Toss the dressing with the salad. Garnish with pumpkin seeds and crumbled feta.

Cook's Note: Pomegranate molasses, a syruplike reduction of pomegranate juice and sugar, is sold in grocery stores, such as Whole Foods Market, or specialty Middle Eastern stores. Otherwise, substitute 2 tablespoons of balsamic vinegar and use 5 tablespoons of olive oil instead of four (skip adding the water).

Ramen Kale Crunchy Slaw

Jim Feiner's kale slaw is a combination of cabbage, carrot and kale that is colorful, crunchy and tasty—perfect for a party or barbecue. Jim grew up working in a restaurant kitchen, specifically with his father at the Beach Plum Inn and Restaurant on Martha's Vineyard, opened originally by his grandfather. So although he took over the family real estate business here on the island, he remains a very creative cook and has given me a number of good ideas for kale.

- 4 cups kale (about ½ bunch, stripped from stalk, rinsed, cut into ¼-inch ribbons, rinsed and dried)
- 2 teaspoons olive oil
- 2 pinches of kosher salt
- 4 cups thinly shredded cabbage (a mix of red and green cabbages looks great)

- 2 carrots, peeled and shredded
- 1 (2- or 3-ounce) packet ramen noodles
- 3 tablespoons sesame seeds, toasted
- ¼ cup almond slices, toasted

DRESSING

- 3 tablespoons unseasoned rice vinegar
- 2 tablespoons sugar
- ½ teaspoon kosher salt
- 1–2 teaspoons tamari or soy sauce

- ¼ teaspoon freshly ground black pepper
- ¼ cup olive oil
- 2 tablespoons dark sesame oil

1. Place the kale in a large serving bowl or dish and add the olive oil and salt. Massage the kale with your hands to soften and tenderize, about 2 minutes. Add the cabbage and carrots. Crush the ramen noodles in the package and toss with the salad.

2. Make the dressing: In a bowl, combine the vinegar, sugar, salt, tamari, pepper, olive oil and sesame oil and mix well.

3. Add the dressing to the salad 30 to 60 minutes before serving. Toss the dressing evenly to coat and mix in half of the seeds and nuts. Top with the remaining nuts when ready to serve.

Variation: Make this an Asian Chicken Slaw with shredded chicken.

Baby Kale Salad with Strawberries and Feta

Use this salad as a template for fresh fruit in season that can be paired with baby kale. Peaches, nectarines, blackberries, raspberries, watermelon, figs or blueberries all taste great on a kale salad. The hint of sweetness from fresh fruit, including spring strawberries, counterbalanced with mildly salty feta, makes a great topping for baby kale. Ricotta salata or goat cheese can be interchanged, as well as toasted nuts and spiced or sugared nuts.

- 6 cups baby kale (stemmed, rinsed and dried)
- 1 pint strawberries, hulled and sliced
- ½ cup feta cheese, crumbled

WHITE BALSAMIC VINAIGRETTE
- 2 tablespoons white balsamic or strawberry balsamic vinegar (see cook's note)
- 1 tablespoon finely minced shallot
- 5 tablespoons olive oil
- 2 pinches of salt

  Freshly ground black pepper

1. Place the baby kale in a wide salad bowl or platter.

2. Make the dressing: In a small bowl, whisk together the vinegar, shallot and olive oil. Season with the salt and pepper to taste.

3. Just before serving, dress the kale. Top with the sliced strawberries and crumbled feta.

Cook's Note: Other balsamic vinegars can be substituted, all adding their own imprint. I originally created this salad using a strawberry balsamic vinegar from Gustare, a favorite oil and vinegar shop on Cape Cod where I've done food demos and spent time taste testing its many varieties. Gustare's fruit vinegars especially—strawberry, raspberry, blueberry, cranberry—are so luscious and flavorful you can usually cut back on the amount of olive oil used. You can read about Gustare's products online at www.gustareoliveoil.com.

Kale Salad with Apple, Dried Cranberries and Feta

This salad created by Jacqueline Foster won first prize at our local kale fest at Mermaid Farm on Martha's Vineyard. At the time, Jackee was cheese maker at the farm, which had an abundance of winter kale. We offered kale cooking classes in barns and hoop houses, took people on tours to learn about winter kale growing, and planned to crown a kale king and queen based on the best dishes. We ended up with three crowned queens and a great kale brunch, including this winning salad. Jackee now makes cheese at the nearby Grey Barn and Farm in Chilmark, Massachusetts.

- 1 large bunch kale, stripped from stalk, sliced into very thin strips, rinsed and dried (about 12 leaves, or 6 cups)
- 1 tablespoon olive oil
- 2 pinches of kosher salt
- ¼ cup dried cranberries, roughly chopped
- ¼ cup toasted sunflower seeds
- 1 crisp apple, cored and diced small
- ½ cup crumbled Mermaid Farm feta cheese

DRESSING

- 1 tablespoon cider vinegar
- 2 tablespoons olive oil

1. In a large bowl, mix the kale with the olive oil and salt, and massage for 2 to 3 minutes. This breaks down the fibers and releases some of the bitter flavor.

2. Add the cranberries, sunflower seeds and apple.

3. Make the dressing: Mix the vinegar with the olive oil. Toss the salad with your desired amount of dressing. Top with the feta.

Carnival Kale Salad

This salad has crunch, sweetness and a giant bowlful of colorful vegetables. Perfect to bring to someone's house for a potluck or as a workday lunch for a few days. Baby kale is sold in grocery stores, and increasingly at farmers' markets. If unavailable, try massaging larger kale leaves as a substitute, see page 30.

- 3 cups lightly packed baby kale (stemmed, roughly chopped or sliced, and rinsed and dried)
- 2 cups red cabbage, sliced as thinly as you can
- 2 carrots, peeled and shredded (about 1 cup)
- 1 crisp apple, such as Braeburn
- 1 lemon wedge
- ½ cup dried cranberries, roughly chopped
- 1½ cups shelled frozen edamame
- ½ cup sunflower seeds or sliced almonds, toasted

CIDER HONEY DRESSING

- 2 tablespoons cider vinegar
- 1½ teaspoons honey
- 2 teaspoons finely minced shallot (optional)
- 6 tablespoons olive oil
- 2 good pinches of salt

1. Mix the kale, cabbage and carrots in a wide bowl or platter. Core and finely dice the apple and drizzle with a squeeze of lemon juice to keep from browning. Add to the salad.

2. Prepare the edamame (which already come precooked) by placing them in a colander and pouring a kettle of boiling water over them. Let cool. Add to the salad, along with the cranberries.

3. Make the dressing: In a small bowl, whisk together the vinegar, honey, shallot, if using, and olive oil. Season with the salt. Just before serving, add the dressing to the salad and mix well. Toss with the sunflower seeds. (Or only mix the portion of the salad you will be eating that day.)

Radicchio and Kale Salad

I wasn't expecting to create a salad with radicchio, until grower Zephir Plume of Martha's Vineyard gave me a perfect head she had grown and I realized how nicely it contrasted with the deep green kale. I added a few torn petals of edible nasturtium flowers from the garden—which made the salad look so good it was fit for company. Sometimes store-bought radicchio can be too bitter—taste a tiny bit of a leaf before you purchase. This salad is meant for tender, baby kale; I'd suggest another salad if it's unavailable.

- 1 small head radicchio, or ½ larger head (about 1½ cups)
- 6 cups baby kale (stemmed, rinsed and dried)
- 6 edible nasturtium flowers (if available), torn into smaller pieces
- 1 just-ripe avocado, pitted and sliced
- 2 tablespoons pecorino or Parmesan cheese

LEMON DRESSING

- 2 tablespoons fresh lemon juice
- 1 garlic clove, finely minced, or 1 tablespoon minced shallot
- 6 tablespoons olive oil
- 2 good pinches of kosher salt
  Freshly ground black pepper

1. Cut the radicchio into quarters, remove the core, and slice into fairly thin strips. In a wide salad bowl or platter, combine the baby kale and radicchio. Place some nasturtium petals on top.

2. Make the dressing: Combine the lemon juice, garlic, olive oil, salt and pepper in a small bowl. Just before serving, shake or whisk the dressing and use your desired amount on the salad. (You will have some dressing left over.) Gently toss in the avocado slices and pecorino cheese and mix lightly.

Apple-Walnut and Other Variations: You could try adding a crisp apple, sliced very thinly, along with some toasted walnuts to this salad, for variety. Add the apple just before dressing, to prevent discoloring. Or try fresh sliced pears or roasted pears, nuts and cheese with the kale and radicchio. Change up the cheese with ricotta salata, goat cheese or feta. Add thinly sliced red onions instead of garlic in the dressing. Dried cranberries or apricots also can be added.

Grilled Kale and Tomato Panzanella Salad

This trio comes together so easily, perfect for a summer of night of grilling to accompany grilled steak, fish or chicken. This idea for grilled kale and panzanella salad comes from friend and cookbook author Karen Covey, whose new book, *The Coastal Table*, includes 120 recipes inspired by farms and the seacoast of southern New England.

½ French baguette (wider baguette is best) or sourdough loaf

Olive oil

Salt and freshly ground black pepper

1 bunch curly kale (8 to 10 ounces, 10 to 12 stalks)

2–3 fresh tomatoes, cut into bite-size chunks

DRESSING

1 tablespoon fresh lemon juice

1 small garlic clove, finely minced

2 tablespoons chopped fresh basil

3 tablespoons olive oil

Salt and freshly ground black pepper

1. Preheat a grill to medium.

2. Slice the baguette into thick slices, about ¾ inch, and place on a baking sheet. Brush with olive oil on both sides, then season with salt and pepper.

3. Rinse the kale. Place the leaves on a sheet tray lined with paper towels to dry off the leaves. Leave the kale on the stalk to help with grilling. Brush the leaves with about 1 tablespoon of oil, and rub into all the crevices with your hands. Season with salt. Add a bit more oil, if needed.

4. Oil the grill well. Place the kale leaves on the grates, opening the leaves flat. Grill for about 2 minutes on each side, until lightly charred. The kale will still be green, cooked to a texture between crispy and soft.

5. Grill the baguette slices on both sides, until lightly crisp, 3 to 4 minutes.

6. Place the tomato chunks on a platter. With scissors or a knife, cut the kale leaves away from the stalk and cut or tear into bite-size pieces. Add to the tomatoes.

7. Make the dressing: In a small bowl, whisk together all the dressing ingredients. Add the desired amount of dressing to the kale salad and mix well. Tear or cut the grilled bread into smaller pieces and add to the salad. Gently mix in. Serve immediately.

Chris Fischer's Kale Caesar Salad

I would always make a point to attend any community dinner or event on Martha's Vineyard where Chris was cooking—there was sure to be kale and other impeccably fresh Island meat, fish and vegetables. Now Chris is running the Beach Plum Restaurant and getting lots of press, while continuing to farm his family's land at Beetlebung Corner to supply the restaurant. He suggests getting the dressing in every nook and cranny of the kale leaf, and topping the salad with toasted bread crumbs or croutons.

1 pound kale, stripped off stalk and torn into pieces	3 anchovy fillets
Salt	Freshly ground black pepper
4 tablespoons canola or olive oil, divided	1 garlic clove, roughly chopped
2 egg yolks	Bread crumbs or croutons, for garnish (to make croutons, see page 45)
½ tablespoon Dijon mustard	
2 tablespoons lemon juice	

1. Wash the kale thoroughly by soaking in water repeatedly until the water is clean when the kale is removed. Spin dry in a salad spinner and place in a large bowl. Salt the kale lightly and drizzle 1 tablespoon of the canola oil into a bowl. Toss and massage salt and oil into the kale vigorously, until well coated.

2. In a blender, combine the egg yolks, mustard, lemon juice, anchovies, pepper and garlic. Puree until you have a smooth paste. You may need to add a small amount of cold water to loosen up mixture at this point. Add the remaining 3 tablespoons of oil to the blender while pulsing to incorporate it. When you have a cohesive dressing, transfer it to a measuring cup or bowl.

3. An hour before serving, pour half of the dressing onto the kale and massage vigorously again to coat evenly. Add more dressing, if desired, as well as salt and pepper to taste. Reserve the remaining dressing for another use. Enjoy!

Cook's Note: Try this dressing with baby kale, too, if it's available. You can just add the baby kale to a salad bowl and toss with some of the Caesar dressing—there's no need for prior massaging, as baby kale is tender to begin with.

Summer Peach and Baby Kale Salad

This salad is nice for company, especially with flavorful juicy peaches we are sometimes lucky to find at the market. The salad also features fresh mozzarella marinated in lemon, garlic and basil. The marinade/dressing, along with the mozzarella, is then poured over the baby kale and sliced peaches. Easy and delicious.

LEMON BASIL MARINADE/DRESSING

- 1 teaspoon lemon zest
- 1 tablespoon fresh lemon juice
- 4 tablespoons olive oil
- 1 garlic clove, finely minced
- ¼ teaspoon red pepper flakes
- 2 pinches kosher salt

    Freshly ground black pepper

SALAD

- 6–8 basil leaves, thinly sliced
- 1 (8-ounce) container small, fresh mozzarella balls, cut in half or into quarters
- 5–6 cups baby kale (stemmed, rinsed and dried)
- 1 large or 2 medium-size juicy, ripe peaches or nectarines

1. Make the marinade/dressing: In a medium-size bowl, combine the lemon zest, lemon juice, olive oil, garlic, red pepper flakes, salt and pepper.

2. Add the basil and mozzarella and let sit for 10 to 15 minutes (longer is okay, too).

3. Place the baby kale in a wide salad bowl. Just before serving, pour the mozzarella and all the marinade/dressing onto the kale salad and toss gently with tongs. Peel the peaches and slice fairly thinly. (Nectarines don't usually need to be peeled.) Add to the salad, and serve immediately.

Or anytime. Regular curly kale, perhaps with a little of the lacinato kale mixed in, makes a nice base for the raspberries, pomegranate seeds, juicy orange slices and sliced celery. This salad is a bright accompaniment to any Italian pasta dishes, or to feature alongside fish. It makes a dramatic dish to bring to a potluck, and can easily be doubled.

- 6 cups chopped kale (about 1 bunch, stripped from stalk, chopped into bite-size pieces, rinsed and dried)
- 1 tablespoon olive oil
- 2 pinches of salt
- 1–2 celery stalks, peeled, cut in half lengthwise, and sliced razor thin on an angle
- 3 navel oranges, peeled and segmented or sliced

- into half rounds (see cook's note)
- ½ cup pomegranate seeds (about ½ pomegranate), or ⅓ cup sliced dried apricots or cranberries
- 1 cup fresh raspberries
- 8 pitted dried dates, thinly sliced
- ½ cup sliced almonds, toasted at 350°F for 5 minutes

ORANGE BALSAMIC VINAIGRETTE

- 2 tablespoons balsamic vinegar
- 2 tablespoons fresh orange juice
- 1 tablespoon finely minced shallot
- 1 teaspoon pure maple syrup or honey
- 5 tablespoons olive oil
- 2 good pinches of salt, or to taste

1. Place the kale in a wide salad bowl. Sprinkle with the olive oil and salt. Massage with your hands for 2 to 3 minutes, until the kale is reduced and glistening. You might have about 4 cups. It should taste good. (If it seems moist, use a paper towel to take out some of the moisture.)

2. Make the dressing: Whisk together the vinegar, orange juice, shallot, maple syrup, olive oil and salt in a small bowl.

3. Just before serving, whisk the dressing again, dress the salad with your desired amount of vinaigrette (you may not need it all) and toss with tongs. Top with the celery, orange, pomegranate seeds, raspberries, dates, and finally, the nuts.

Cook's Note: This is a salad ripe for colorful additions or substitutions. Thinly sliced red cabbage or radicchio adds a nice crunch and contrast with the soft oranges. Add some sliced avocado. Buy a just-ripe avocado, not too soft and not rock hard. Slice and add. If you can't find pomegranates or even dates, try thinly sliced dried apricots or cranberries. Red segmented grapefruits could be mixed in with oranges. I've substituted walnuts and pecans, or for the holidays, some homemade spiced or sweetened nuts.

Kale, Apple, Fennel and Goat Cheese

A very simple salad to make with sophisticated flavors. This works best with baby kale that is 2 to 3 inches long. If you have only mature kale, try the massaged kale salad recipe with apples, feta and sunflower seeds.

LEMON APPLE VINAIGRETTE

- 1 tablespoon fresh lemon juice
- 1 tablespoon cider vinegar
- 2 teaspoons honey
- 5 tablespoons olive oil
  Salt

SALAD

- 4 cups baby kale (stemmed, rinsed and dried)
- 1 apple, peeled if desired, cored and very thinly sliced
- 1 cup sliced fennel (about ½ bulb)
- ¼ cup dried cranberries, roughly chopped
  Goat cheese, for garnish

1. Make the dressing: Whisk together the lemon juice, vinegar, honey and olive oil in a small bowl. Season with salt to taste.

2. Place the kale on a platter or wide salad bowl. Add the apple and fennel. Pour your desired amount of dressing into the salad and mix with tongs; top with the cranberries. Just before serving, crumble the goat cheese on top.

Lunch Kale in a Jar

Bring a salad to work and save money. Using a mason jar, the dressing goes at the bottom, followed by kale and vegetables on top. When lunchtime arrives, shake the jar and serve the salad on a plate. The recipe is written with some vegetable suggestions, but add whatever vegetables, beans or leftover chicken you conveniently have in your refrigerator. Feta cheese is always a good choice for any kale salad.

DRESSING

- 2 teaspoons fresh lemon juice
- 1 small garlic clove, pressed in a garlic press
- 2 tablespoons olive oil
- 2 teaspoons mayonnaise
  Salt and freshly ground black pepper

SALAD

- 2 cups baby kale (stemmed, rinsed and dried)
  Grated carrot
- ½ avocado, pitted and sliced
  Sliced cucumber
- ¼ cup shredded red cabbage or thinly sliced red onion (optional)

HEALTHY ADD-ONS

Hard-boiled egg, smoked fish, leftover chicken, beans, arame seaweed, sunflower or pumpkin seeds, walnuts

Whisk the dressing ingredients together in a small bowl and pour into the bottom of a wide-mouth quart-size mason jar. Top with the kale, carrot, avocado, cucumber and cabbage. Place the lid on, and try to keep the jar upright until ready to shake and serve for lunch. Serve the salad on a plate with optional add-ons of your choice after shaking it up.

Sides

Butternut Squash, Kale and Corn

This is an attractive combo of three fall favorites, especially in that period when squash comes to markets, but fresh local Morning Glory Farm corn is still available. If you can't find fresh corn—which does add a nice light crunch—try the Cascadian Farms frozen corn. We love this side dish with seared scallops and a basil or lemon sauce.

½ bunch kale, stripped from stalk, chopped into bite-size pieces, and rinsed (4 to 5 cups)

1 tablespoon olive oil

1 tablespoon butter

1 small butternut squash, peeled, seeded and cut into ½- to ¾-inch dice (3 to 4 cups)

½ teaspoon kosher salt, plus more to taste

2 ears corn, kernels removed from cob (about 1½ cups)

⅛ teaspoon cayenne pepper

¼ teaspoon ground cumin

   Freshly ground black pepper

1 lime, quartered

1. In a large skillet with a lid, bring 3 to 4 cups of water to a boil. Add the kale. Cover and cook over high heat, stirring occasionally, until tender, 4 to 6 minutes, depending on the kale. Drain in a colander, shaking a few times, to release the steam and stop the cooking.

2. Dry the skillet and heat the olive oil and butter over medium heat. (The pan should be large enough to fit the squash in a single layer.) Add the butternut squash and sauté over medium heat, stirring occasionally, until *lightly* browned and cooked without falling apart, about 15 minutes. Add a few pinches of salt while cooking. Add the corn, cayenne, cumin, the ¼ teaspoon of salt and pepper to taste and cook for 4 to 5 additional minutes, until the corn is cooked. When ready to serve, add the kale back to the pan and stir gently to warm. Add another pinch of salt for the kale. Squeeze a little lime juice into the dish or pass lime wedges around for people to squeeze their own.

Roasted Cauliflower and Kale

After roasting together in the oven, the contrasting cauliflower and kale look nice together on a platter, garnished with toasted pine nuts. The brown butter—which takes only a few minutes to make—gives the pair a nutty flavor, but if you can also substitute olive oil, if that's easier. We're not crisping kale here, but going for an intermediary stage of softened, cooked kale. For some added depth, top with some grated Parmesan or Gruyère cheese.

- 3 tablespoons unsalted butter, sliced into tablespoons
- 1 medium-size head of cauliflower cut into uniform, bite-size florets (5 to 6 cups)
- 4 cups curly kale (about ½ bunch, stripped from stalk, chopped or torn into bite-size pieces, rinsed and dried)
- ½ teaspoon kosher salt, plus more for the kale
- ¼ cup pine nuts, toasted

1. Preheat the oven to 425°F. Heat the butter in a small, thick-bottomed stainless-steel skillet over medium heat. Whisk the butter as it foams and continue as the foam begins to disappear and you begin to see brown bits, 3 to 4 minutes. It should smell nutty. Remove from the heat to prevent burning and set aside.

2. Place the cauliflower on a parchment paper–lined baking sheet and drizzle with about 2 tablespoons of the butter. Mix well to coat. Season with the salt and place the cauliflower in the oven, turning at least once during roasting to prevent any side from burning. Set the timer for 15 minutes.

3. Place the kale in a bowl and rub the remaining tablespoon of butter and two pinches of salt into the kale. Try to get all parts of the kale pieces buttered.

4. After the cauliflower has roasted for 15 minutes, lower the oven temperature to 350°F. Push the cauliflower to one side of the baking sheet and add the kale. Continue to roast for another 12 minutes or so, mixing at least once, for a total of about 27 minutes. The cauliflower should be easily pierced with a fork, and the kale softened, pleasantly edible with some pieces being slightly crispy. Times could vary depending on the size of the cut cauliflower.

5. Turn the duo onto a platter, mix together and top with the pine nuts.

Kale with Raisins and Pine Nuts

Serve this side dish to people who say they don't like kale, as a test. It's a winning combination, based on the old Italian classic of greens, a touch of sweetness from a few raisins, garlic and crunch from the pine nuts. Braising the kale first in water softens it pleasantly—I find it better than most kale sautéed directly in the pan.

1 bunch kale, stripped from stalk, chopped into bite-size pieces and rinsed (10 to 12 ounces, 6 to 8 cups)

1 tablespoon olive oil

2 garlic cloves, finely minced

⅓ cup raisins

  Salt

¼ cup pine nuts, toasted

1. Bring about 4 cups of water to a boil in a sauté pan with a lid or a soup pot and add the kale. Cover and cook over high heat, stirring occasionally, until tender, 4 to 6 minutes. Strain in a colander, and shake several times to release the steam to stop the cooking.

2. Dry the same skillet and heat the olive oil over low heat. Add the garlic and raisins and sauté for 1 to 2 minutes, stirring the whole time to prevent the garlic from burning.

3. Add the kale and stir to combine, until the greens are heated through. Season with salt to taste. Serve hot, garnished with the pine nuts.

Sautéed Kale with Mushrooms

Use this recipe for a combination of kale and mushrooms to create lots of different flavor profiles. With soy flavoring, minced ginger tastes good with kale, alongside or instead of the garlic. Or instead of the soy sauce, mix a touch of butter, sour cream, cream and mascarpone with Parmesan, Romano or Gruyère cheese. A touch of sherry, red wine or cognac, cooked off after sautéing the mushroom, adds flavor depth as well. Try fresh garden herbs, such as chives, dill, thyme, rosemary, sage, tarragon and/or scallion, lemon zest and lemon.

6–8 cups kale (about 1 bunch, stripped from stalk, chopped into bite-size pieces and rinsed)

1 tablespoon plus 1 teaspoon olive oil, divided

1 shallot, thinly sliced (about ¼ cup)

8 ounces cremini or mixed wild mushrooms, thinly sliced (about 2 cups)

1 garlic clove, finely minced

Pinch of salt

2 teaspoons soy sauce or tamari

1. Bring about 4 cups of water to a boil in a sauté pan or skillet with a lid and add the kale. Cover and cook over high heat, stirring occasionally, until tender, 4 to 6 minutes. Strain in a colander, and shake several times to release the steam. Set aside.

2. Dry the same skillet and heat 1 tablespoon of the olive oil over medium-low heat. Add the shallot and sauté for about 2 minutes, before adding the mushrooms. Raise the heat to medium and continue to cook until the mushrooms are cooked, stirring often. Add the garlic and stir until fragrant.

3. Add back the kale and stir to combine, until the greens are heated through. Stir in a pinch or two of salt, the soy sauce, and the remaining teaspoon of olive oil. Serve hot.

Variation: Creamed Kale: Give the mushroom kale combo a creamy texture. Instead of the soy sauce at the end, add 1 teaspoon of fresh thyme, 2 tablespoons of half-and-half or cream and 2 tablespoons of Parmigiano-Reggiano cheese. Finish with a grind of black pepper.

Roasted Potatoes and Kale with Cheese

Crispy oven-baked potatoes are topped with cooked kale and flavored with a layer of melted feta or blue cheese. Try this with a grilled steak or hamburgers.

2 pounds red potatoes, peeled and cut into 3¾-inch dice (about 5 medium-size potatoes)

2 tablespoons olive oil

Salt

1 bunch kale, stripped from stalk, chopped into bite-size pieces and rinsed (about 5 cups)

¾ cup blue cheese, Gorgonzola or feta (see cook's note)

1. Preheat the oven to 350°F. Place the potatoes into an ovenproof serving dish (such as a lasagne pan)—it should fill the container in one layer, but not be overcrowded. Add the olive oil and mix well; sprinkle with salt. Bake, flipping over a few times, until the potatoes are golden and easily pierced with a fork, 40 to 50 minutes, depending on the size of the dice.

2. While the potatoes are baking, bring 4 or 5 cups of water to a boil in a wide pot with a lid. Boil the kale, covered, stirring once, for 5 or 6 minutes, until tender. Pour into a strainer—shake the strainer several times to release the steam. When cool, squeeze out any excess water and set aside.

3. When the potatoes are done, spread the kale over the potatoes and add a pinch or two of salt over the top of the kale. Distribute the cheese over the top, and place back in the oven for 10 minutes, until hot and the cheese is melted.

Cook's Note: Blue cheese tastes delicious with beef. You may have your favorite, but mine is Great Hill Blue Cheese, for those who live in the New England area. For a flavorful feta, I recommend the Valbreso French sheep's milk (found in most Whole Foods Markets and other supermarkets, as well as the Greek sheep's milk–goat's milk combo. A nice brand is Mt. Vikos.

THE KALE CHRONICLES

How to Create a Recipe If You Aren't a Cook

During the last six months of 2013, we had many family members visiting and staying with us. My husband's 93-year-old mother was living with us part of the year and relatives came to visit Justine and help out. All of them joined in the process of testing kale recipes and giving feedback.

One of them was Merrie, David's niece, who lived with us for three months. She had grown up not cooking much, and definitely not eating or enjoying many vegetables. She would be a perfect tester for kale dishes, a nonbeliever. If Merrie liked them, I would consider myself on the right track at least. Plus, she hoped to get in shape and eat better while she was here and in between jobs.

She did have the task of cooking lunches for Dave's mom and, one week, in the course of this, asked me to buy a head of cauliflower. The cauliflower sat in the fridge unused. I finally asked her when she was going to use it—as I had spent nearly seven dollars on it at our island grocery store. "Tonight," she answered. "Okay," I said, "let's do a test with kale—maybe roasting it; that's usually a good treatment for cauliflower." Kale and cauliflower would probably go well together,

I thought, as kale goes well with many "white" ingredients, including pasta, white beans, potatoes, lending its stronger flavor to the milder white ingredient.

I gave Merrie the job of figuring out what flavorings or aromatics to use. I handed her *The Flavor Bible: The Essential Guide to Culinary Creativity*, by Karen Page and Andrew Dorneburg. This is a favorite resource of mine, often sparking ideas for recipes. It lists each ingredient alphabetically—artichokes to watercress—and all the foods that taste best with that particular ingredient. Merrie took the book to the couch. A while later she came back with her ideas: nutmeg, brown butter and pine nuts.

"I think they'll all work, except nutmeg," I said.

Merrie frowned. "How will you know, unless you try?"

I couldn't argue with that.

I asked Merrie to look up on the Internet and tell me how long we should brown the butter for it. She came back with the basic timing.

I showed her a good technique for cutting the cauliflower florets. If you cut through the stem, but not all the way through the floret and gently pull it apart, it keeps its rounded appearance and is more natural looking.

We set the oven to 425°F. Of course, I had made crispy kale in the oven, but never roasted kale as a side dish. I had been wondering, however, about the flavor of kale in that intermediary stage where it's half-cooked, a bit reduced, yet not crisped.

We browned three tablespoons of butter and poured two tablespoons over the cauliflower, added a couple of pinches of salt, and started roasting that first, on a baking sheet. We mixed the other tablespoon of butter with the torn kale leaves and set that aside. After halfway through the cooking, we pushed the cauliflower to one side of the cooking sheet and added the kale.

When both came out, we transferred them to a serving dish and added some toasted pine nuts. The pair looked beautiful together. We brought a nutmeg and a grater to the table. We sat down to sample that along with a kale Caesar salad and some chicken.

It worked.

"You've created your first recipe," I told Merrie. "We'll have to see what the testers think."

I added a sprinkling of lemon juice to see whether it elevated the flavor. No. Then a few currants, not bad. A grating of Gruyère cheese. That was delicious, and became a variation.

Then Merrie grated a little nutmeg on our cauliflower and kale.

"Nope," we said in unison.

Addendum: The testers loved the combination, and it sparked more tests. When I told one tester, Linda London-Thompson, that I was going to try roasting carrots and kale next, she thought parsnips would taste great. And she suggested making a yogurt sauce to accompany it. I used carrots and parsnips with the kale, in the same manner, using cumin in the first test, and curry in subsequent tests. The combination with the yogurt was amazing—cooling and contrasting. Thank you, Linda—that's something I wouldn't have thought of.

Melted Leeks and Kale

This is an all-purpose kale sauté, particularly good as a side with chicken, beef or fish, such as halibut or salmon.

1 large bunch kale, stripped from stalk, chopped and rinsed (8 to 10 cups)

1 tablespoon oil

3 tablespoons butter, divided

2 large whole leeks, trimmed, cut in half lengthwise,

rinsed and sliced (3 to 4 cups)

1 cup white wine

Salt and freshly ground black pepper

Lemon wedge

1. In a sauté pan with a lid, bring at least 4 cups of water to a boil. Add the kale and precook it for 4 to 6 minutes, until tender, mixing once or twice. Drain, and shake the colander to release the steam. Set aside.

2. Dry the same skillet and heat the olive oil and 1 tablespoon of the butter on medium-low heat. Add the leeks and sauté for about 10 minutes, stirring occasionally. Add the wine, cover, and simmer for 8 to 10 minutes, until the wine is nearly gone.

3. Melt the remaining 2 tablespoons of butter into the leeks. Add the kale back to reheat and season with salt and pepper. Serve hot, with a light squeeze of lemon juice.

Two-Minute Garlic Kale

The dark, earthy Italian kale works nicely here because the flatter strips of leaves can be easily slivered, though any kale will do. Serve with the steak, chicken, meat loaf—anything where a lot of other flavors are going on and you want a simple kale side.

6 cups kale (about 1 bunch, stripped from stalk and rinsed)

2 tablespoons olive oil

1–2 teaspoons finely minced garlic

Salt

1 lemon wedge

1. Pile four or five kale leaves together flatly and then roll into a loose "cigar." With a knife, cut strips ⅛ to ¼ inch wide.

2. Heat a skillet over medium heat until hot, so the kale will sizzle. Add the oil, kale and garlic. Using a pair of tongs, continually lift the kale, like stir-frying, for about 2 minutes, until tender. Season with salt. Just before serving, add a squeeze of lemon juice.

Quick Sauté of Broccoli, Kale and Red Cabbage

SERVES 4

This new favorite is a super quick and gorgeous-looking side that can accompany a wide range of dinners. All three ingredients can be cooked together in less than ten minutes, using a bit of ginger and garlic as an accent.

- 2 cups broccoli florets
- 2 tablespoons olive, peanut or coconut oil
- 3 cups kale, stripped from stalk, thinly sliced, and rinsed
- 2 cups red cabbage, thinly sliced
- 1 teaspoon finely minced garlic
- 2 teaspoons finely minced fresh ginger
- Salt

1. Cut the broccoli into small florets—think of a bite-size floret and then cut that into quarters. You want them small enough to cook quickly.

2. Pour your oil of choice into a large, heavy-bottomed skillet. Add the broccoli and stir-fry on medium to medium-high heat for about 3 minutes, stirring constantly. Add the kale and red cabbage, continuing to stir (tongs work nicely here) for about 3 minutes. Add the garlic and ginger, lower the heat, and continue to sauté for about 1 minute longer, until the kale and cabbage are tender. Add salt to taste.

Kale, Leeks and Bacon

SERVES 4

A tasty, easy combo.

- 4 slices uncooked bacon
- 1 tablespoon olive oil
- 1 whole leek, trimmed, cut in half lengthwise and sliced
- 6–8 cups kale (about 1 bunch, stripped from stalk, chopped into bite-size pieces, rinsed but not dried)
- 1 cup corn kernels (stripped from 1 to 2 ears corn)
- Salt and freshly ground black pepper
- 1 teaspoon cider vinegar

1. Fry the bacon until cooked. Drain on a paper towel, let cool and crumble. Discard the fat.

2. In a large sauté pan with a lid, heat the olive oil and leek over medium heat. Sauté for about 5 minutes, stirring often. Add the kale with the water still clinging to the leaves, turn the heat to medium-high, and sauté until wilted, about 2 minutes. Cover, lower the heat to medium or medium-low and continue to cook the kale for another 3 minutes. If at any point the mixture is dry and sticking to the pan, add a few tablespoons of water. Add the corn, mix well, and continue to cook for another 2 minutes.

3. Season with salt, a bit of pepper and the vinegar. Stir well. Serve hot, garnished with the crumbled bacon.

Sautéed Fall Kale and Apples

This is a recipe your whole family will love—it's so simple to make and it goes especially well with roast chicken or on the holiday table. Shallots, quicker cooking than onions, cook along with sautéed diced apples. That hint of sweetness is just what kale often needs.

- 1 bunch kale, stripped from stalk, chopped into bite-size pieces and rinsed (10 to 12 ounces, 6 to 8 cups)
- 1 tablespoon butter
- 2 medium-size shallots, thinly sliced (about ½ cup)
- 2 crisp apples, such as Braeburn or Granny Smith, cored, peeled and cut into ½-inch dice
- 2 teaspoons brown sugar
- ¼ cup dried cranberries, roughly chopped
  Salt
- 2 teaspoons olive oil
- ⅓ cup walnuts, toasted and chopped (optional)

1. Place about 4 cups of water in a 10- or 12-inch skillet or soup pot that has a tight-fitting lid. Bring to a boil and add the kale. Cover and cook over high heat, stirring occasionally, until tender, 4 to 6 minutes, depending on the kale. Transfer to a colander to drain. Shake a few times to release the steam and stop the cooking.

2. Dry the skillet and melt the butter over medium-low heat. Add the shallots and apples and sauté until the apples are nicely colored and nearly soft, 5 to 7 minutes. Add the brown sugar and cranberries and sauté for a few minutes more.

3. Add the cooked kale (squeeze out any excess moisture), a pinch or two of salt and the olive oil and mix well. Top with the walnuts, if using, and serve hot.

Cook's Note: Try this also with pears, or a combination of apples and pears.

Indian-Inspired Warm Kale Sauté

Make sure your curry powder is fresh—taste a tiny bit on your tongue to make sure it's not bitter. You can also vary this side dish in a number of ways—making it simpler with kale and ginger; adding more vegetables, such as roasted potatoes or cauliflower; or even combining it with a bit of canned coconut milk.

1 bunch kale, stripped from stalk, chopped into bite-size pieces and rinsed (6 to 8 cups)

1½ tablespoons canola, coconut, or peanut oil or butter

1 large shallot, thinly sliced (about ¼ cup)

1 cup shredded carrot (2 medium carrots)

¼ cup raisins or currants

2 teaspoons grated fresh ginger

1½ teaspoons mild curry powder

Salt

1. In a skillet with a lid, bring 4 cups water to a boil and cook the kale for 4 to 6 minutes, or until tender. Drain, and shake the colander until all the steam is gone. Set aside.

2. In the same skillet, heat your oil of choice over low heat and sauté the shallot for about 2 minutes. Add the carrot and sauté for another 2 to 3 minutes longer, until the shallot is golden. Add the raisins, ginger and curry and sauté for another minute or so. Add the kale to reheat, along with two pinches of salt. Mix well and taste to see if you need any adjustments.

Mashed Potatoes with Kale

Kale and mashed potatoes is a match made in—Ireland. There, it is a traditional dish called colcannon. No matter how you approach this combination—with additions of scallions, garlic, cabbage, butter, no butter—it's a dish of pure comfort. Serve with meatloaf, roast chicken—anytime you need mashed potatoes, plus. I love it made with both kale and either regular cabbage or even better, savoy cabbage.

- 2 pounds potatoes, peeled and cut into chunks
- 1 tablespoon olive oil
- 3 tablespoons butter, divided
- 1 leek, cut in half lengthwise, rinsed and cut into ¼-inch slices
- 2 cups savoy or green cabbage, thinly sliced
- 3 cups chopped kale (stripped from stalk, cut into small bite-size pieces, rinsed and dried)
  Salt
- ½ cup milk (optional)

1. Bring a pot of water to a boil and start cooking the potatoes.

2. While the potatoes are cooking, heat the olive oil and 1 tablespoon of the butter in a large skillet and sauté the leek until wilted, 5 to 8 minutes. Add the cabbage and cook until wilted, 2 to 3 minutes more. Add 1½ cups of water, bring to a boil, and then lower the heat and simmer for 5 minutes. Add the kale and a few pinches of salt and continue to cook on medium-low heat, covered, for another 5 minutes, or until the kale and cabbage are cooked. There should be a little water left, which you can drain and reserve to use in the mashed potatoes instead of milk.

3. When the potatoes are cooked, drain and mash with a masher, ricer or hand mixer. Add up to 1½ cups of the cooking water or milk and the remaining 2 tablespoons of butter. Season well with salt. This is a subtle dish and needs salt to bring out the flavors.

4. Combine the mashed potatoes and the kale mixture in an ovenproof dish or deep-dish pie plate. Reheat in a 350°F oven, either with foil or uncovered if you like your potatoes crusty, until hot, 15 to 20 minutes. (This can also be prepared ahead of time and reheated in the oven.)

Roasted Curried Carrots, Parsnips and Kale

Roasting kale—before it turns crispy—is an easy way to prepare it as a side dish. The accompanying carrots and parsnips add a hint of sweetness and color. A bit of yogurt on the side makes it delectable. Don't miss this dish because you don't like curry—it is easily made with other spices and herbs, or even just olive oil and salt, because the vegetables are so flavorful, see the cook's note below.

- 2 cups carrots (peeled and cut like French fries into 2 x ½-inch sticks)
- 2 cups parsnips (peeled and cut like French fries into 2 x ½-inch sticks)
- 3 tablespoons olive oil, divided

- 1 teaspoon mild curry powder
- Salt
- 4 cups kale (about ½ bunch, stripped from stalk, torn into bite-size pieces and rinsed)

YOGURT SAUCE

- ½ cup plain Greek or whole milk yogurt
- 1 teaspoon fresh lemon juice
- ¼ teaspoon dried cumin

- 1 small garlic clove, finely minced
- Salt and freshly ground black pepper

1. Preheat the oven to 400°F. Place the carrot and parsnip in a bowl with 2 tablespoons of the olive oil and the curry. Mix well and sprinkle with salt. Transfer the mixture to a parchment paper–lined baking sheet and bake for 20 minutes, mixing once with tongs during this time.

2. Meanwhile, place the kale in a bowl. Add the remaining tablespoon of oil and two pinches of salt and massage the kale for 1 to 2 minutes with your hands, rubbing the oil on all parts of the kale to begin to tenderize it.

3. Lower the oven temperature to 350°F.

4. When 20 minutes are up, move the baked mixture to one side, and put the kale on the other side. Bake for another 12 to 14 minutes, until the kale has softened and the other vegetables are roasted. Again, mix the kale with tongs once during roasting. A few pieces of the kale may get crunchy, but mostly the kale will be softened enough to enjoy.

5. Make the yogurt sauce: Mix together the yogurt, lemon juice, cumin, garlic and salt and pepper to taste. Serve the vegetables hot on a platter with the yogurt sauce in a small bowl to spoon from.

Variations: Vary the spices on the vegetables, to coincide with the meal it accompanies. About 1 teaspoon of cumin is a nice flavoring for carrots and parsnips, as is a combination of coriander and cumin. Rosemary and thyme can also be used. This dish can also be served without any yogurt sauce as well, although I was surprised at what the yogurt brings to the vegetables.

Soups

Asian Kale Noodle Soup

Thick, toothy Asian noodles in a ginger- and soy-flavored broth paired with kale and mushrooms is pure comfort food—healthy comfort food. I use Nasoya brand fresh Japanese udon noodles, usually found in the dairy section of Whole Foods Market, and created this soup to enjoy them. There's probably not enough protein in the soup to make it a whole meal, but you could easily add something like cooked chicken, tofu or beef.

1 (9-ounce) package Japanese udon noodles

2 tablespoons toasted sesame oil, divided

1 leek, cut in half, rinsed and sliced (about 1½ cups)

1½ cups cremini, shiitake or wild mushrooms, stemmed and sliced

1 teaspoon fresh minced garlic

8 cups chicken stock

3 cups kale (stripped from stalk, chopped and rinsed)

1 carrot, peeled and cut into matchsticks (about 1 cup)

3 tablespoons soy sauce

½ teaspoon kosher salt

¼ teaspoon garlic chili or hot sauce

1 tablespoon grated fresh ginger

1 lime, cut into wedges

1. Cook the noodles according to the package instructions. Drain and shake a few times to release the steam. Drizzle with 1 tablespoon of the sesame oil to keep the noodles from sticking. Set aside.

2. Heat the other tablespoon of oil in a soup pot and sauté the leek and mushrooms over medium heat, until the leek is softened and the mushrooms are cooked, 6 to 7 minutes. Add the garlic and sauté for another 30 to 60 seconds.

3. Add the stock and bring to a boil. Add the kale, and lower the heat to a simmer. Cook, partially covered, for 8 to 10 minutes, until very tender. Add the carrot and cook for 2 to 3 minutes more.

4. Season with the soy sauce, salt and chili sauce. Squeeze the grated ginger and let the ginger juice fall into the soup. (Discard the ginger pulp.)

5. Distribute the noodles among four bowls. Ladle the soup over the noodles. Pass with wedges of lime.

Cook's Note and Variations: For added protein, add shredded chicken or firm tofu. Try dried porcini or shiitake mushrooms and some of the soaking water to give the broth an even richer, fuller taste. I've tried between ¼ and ½ cup of dried mushrooms, rehydrated with 2 cups of boiling water. Chop the mushrooms well after hydrating and add with the stock.

Tortilla, Shrimp and Kale Soup

This is a whole meal in one that comes together fairly quickly. The idea came from Laura Roosevelt, a photographer, writer, poet and friend from Martha's Vineyard, who made a similar version and alerted me to this great combination. She simmered shrimp and kale in a seasoned chicken broth, topped with avocado, tomato, crispy tortilla strips and a squeeze of lime juice. Serve with a salad and enjoy.

- 6 corn tortillas
- 3 tablespoons olive oil, divided
- Salt
- 1 large whole leek, trimmed, cut in half lengthwise, rinsed and sliced into half-rounds
- 2 celery stalks, diced
- 1 red bell pepper, cored and diced
- 1 tablespoon minced garlic (2 large cloves)
- 1 teaspoon ground cumin
- 2 teaspoons chili powder

- 2 teaspoons chipotle peppers in adobo (see cook's note)
- 7 cups chicken stock
- 1 (28-ounce) can diced tomatoes
- 1 bunch lacinato kale stripped from stalk, cut into thin strips and rinsed (½ pound, about 4 cups)
- 2 cups corn kernels (stripped from 2 ears corn)
- 1½ pounds small shrimp, peeled and deveined (larger shrimp can be cut into smaller pieces)
- 1 cup fresh cilantro leaves, coarsely chopped

TOPPINGS

- 1 avocado, pitted and diced
- 2 cups shredded cheese, Cheddar, Monterey Jack or a Mexican blend

- 1 lime, cut into wedges

1. Preheat the oven to 350°F. Cut tortillas in half, then cut each half into ¼-inch strips. Place on a baking sheet; drizzle with 1 tablespoon of the olive oil and a sprinkle of salt. Bake until lightly crisped, turning occasionally with tongs, for 10 to 12 minutes, or until crispy. Set aside.

2. In a soup pot, heat the remaining 2 tablespoons of the olive oil and sauté the leek, celery and red pepper until soft, about 5 minutes. (If you happen to substitute onion for the leek, sauté the trio for at least 10 minutes.) Add the garlic, spices and chipotle pepper and cook for another minute or two. Season with salt as you are cooking.

3. Add the stock and tomatoes and bring to a boil. Add the kale and simmer for 5 minutes. Add the corn and shrimp and simmer on low heat for another 5 minutes. Remove from the heat or serve immediately, so the shrimp doesn't overcook. Taste, and season with additional salt and ¼ cup of chopped cilantro.

4. Arrange the toppings—tortilla strips, diced avocado, cheese and lime—in small bowls. Ladle the soup into soup bowls and pass the toppings around. Don't forget the squeeze of lime juice; it enlivens the soup.

Cook's Note: Chipotles in adobo are sold small cans, found with other Mexican items in the supermarket. Chipotles are smoked jalapeños. *En adobo* means they are stored in a sauce, usually tomato based. They are very spicy, and only a small amount is usually needed. Remove one or two peppers from the can, discard some of the seeds, and chop finely. The flavor takes time to disperse in the soup, so wait awhile before deciding whether or not to add more heat. You can always add more spice; it's difficult to tone down if too spicy. On another note, for a time-saver, use tortilla chips as a garnish instead of baking the corn tortillas.

Cream of Kale Soup

Kale has a natural affinity with potatoes, which also help make this soup creamy without cream. Celery root is added for its bright flavor, but if you can't find it, substitute two celery stalks, two carrots, or just increase the potatoes to three. This is a subtle soup, and it does need a fair amount of salt—add a bit at a time until the flavors of the ingredients emerge. The Gruyère cheese elevates the flavor even more.

- 2 tablespoons butter
- 1 large onion, diced (about 2 cups)
- 2 whole leeks, trimmed, cut lengthwise, rinsed and sliced (3 to 4 cups)
- 2 garlic cloves, minced
- 6 cups water
- 1 small celery root, outside pared away, diced small (about 1½ cups)

- 2 medium-size potatoes, peeled, and diced (about 2 cups)
- 1½ teaspoons salt, plus more to taste
- 5 cups kale, stripped from stalk, chopped into small bite-size pieces, and rinsed (medium-size bunch)
- Gruyère cheese
- Freshly ground black pepper

1. In a soup pot, heat the butter and sauté the onion over medium heat until golden, about 10 minutes. Add the leeks and sauté until softened, another 5 minutes, stirring occasionally. Add the garlic and stir until fragrant, about 1 minute.

2. Add the water and the celery root, potatoes, and salt and bring to a boil. Lower the heat to low, cover, and simmer for about 15 minutes, or until the potatoes are soft.

3. Puree about 3 cups of the soup in a blender, carefully (see the note below about blending hot soup), until creamy or use a stick blender. Return the puree to the pot.

4. Add the kale, bring to a boil, then cover and simmer on low heat until the kale is cooked, about 10 minutes. Stir occasionally; add a small amount of water if the soup is too thick. Check the seasoning and add salt, a bit at a time, tasting as you go, until the leek flavor shines through. (Your salt guide: If the soup tastes bland, add more salt.) Place the soup in the bowls and grate Gruyère cheese to taste over the top. Add some freshly ground black pepper.

Cook's Note: Be careful when blending hot soup—steam buildup can force open the blender lid. When adding hot liquid to a blender, fill it just two-thirds full. Put a towel over the top of the blender and hold it firmly. Blend from low to high speed to prevent steam from pushing the top off.

Chicken Noodle Soup with Kale

Adding kale along with a Parmesan rind dropped in the soup and bit of garlic for an Italian flair turns chicken soup into a luscious treat, especially topped with a spoonful of Parmesan cheese. The orecchiette ("little ear") pasta gives the soup a toothsome texture, perfect for making this a dinner in itself. I occasionally roast two whole chickens, using leftovers for stock to freeze and have on hand for an easy chicken noodle and kale soup like this one.

2 tablespoons olive oil, divided

1 onion, diced

2 garlic cloves, finely minced

8 cups chicken stock

1 Parmesan rind (see cook's note)

2 celery stalks, diced

3 carrots, peeled and diced (about 1½ cups)

Salt

3 cups kale (about ½ bunch, stripped from stalks, chopped into bite-size pieces and rinsed)

2 cups roasted chicken (see page 48 for quick roasting), diced or shredded into medium pieces

8 ounces orecchiette pasta

Parmigiano-Reggiano cheese, for garnish

1. In a soup pot on medium-high heat, sauté the onion in the olive oil for 8 to 10 minutes, stirring often. Add the garlic and sauté for another 30 seconds, stirring to keep it from browning. Add the stock, Parmesan rind, celery, carrots and salt, bring to a boil, then lower the heat and simmer for about 10 minutes.

2. Add the kale and continue to simmer, partially covered, for another 10 to 15 minutes, until tender.

3. Meanwhile, fill a medium-size saucepan with water and bring to a boil. Cook the pasta according to the package instructions. Drain, shake to release the steam, and add a little olive oil to keep the pasta from sticking. Shake again to distribute.

4. When the kale is cooked (try a piece), add the chicken. Check for additional seasoning. If the soup tastes bland, simply add more salt and watch the flavors pop. Remove and discard the Parmesan rind. Ladle the soup, and pass the Parmesan.

Cook's Note: Keep a supply of Parmesan rinds in the freezer (see page 42). Also, as a variation, add chickpeas to the soup.

Kale and Farro Soup

Farro, an Italian whole wheat grain, adds heartiness to this kale and vegetable soup. It also cooks faster than traditional barley, which makes this an easy, quick soup to make. To create a vegetarian version of this soup, add water instead of stock plus two Parmesan rinds.

- 2 tablespoons olive oil
- 1 medium-size onion, diced
- 1 whole leek, all parts, cut in half lengthwise, rinsed and sliced
- 2 medium-size garlic cloves, minced
- 8 cups chicken stock
- 2 large carrots, sliced into half-moons (about 2 cups)
- 2 celery stalks, diced
- 1 tablespoon chopped fresh thyme, or 1 teaspoon dried
- ½ cup farro, rinsed (see cook's note)
- 1–2½ teaspoons kosher salt, divided
- 4 cups kale (½ bunch, stripped from stalk, chopped into bite-size pieces and rinsed)
- 1 (14-ounce) can diced tomatoes, with juices
- Freshly ground black pepper
- Parmesan cheese

1. In a soup pot, heat the olive oil and sauté the onion over medium heat for 4 to 5 minutes, stirring occasionally. Add the leek and sauté until the leek is softened, about 4 minutes. Add the garlic and sauté for another 1 to 2 minutes. Add the stock, carrots, celery, thyme, farro and 1 teaspoon of salt and bring to a boil. Lower the heat to low and simmer the soup, partially covered, for 15 minutes.

2. Stir in the kale and tomatoes. Bring to a boil again, lower the heat to low and simmer for a final 15 to 20 minutes, until the farro is tender. Taste the soup and add additional salt—I used about 2½ teaspoons of kosher salt in all—and a few grinds of pepper. Top each bowl with Parmesan cheese to taste, for more depth of flavor.

Cook's Note: Farro is sometimes found in the dried pasta section, and sometimes with the grains. If you can't find farro, use barley instead. Decrease the amount to ⅓ cup of barley and increase the total cooking time by 15 to 20 minutes for a total of 50 minutes.

Italian White Bean and Kale Soup

If you quick-soak dried beans before making this soup, you can enjoy the creaminess and true taste of a bean, especially the creaminess of the Italian cannellini bean. Any type of kale works here, but the Tuscan or lacinato kale is almost made for soups, it becomes so tender. The recipes calls for water for vegetarians, but using a chicken stock would work, as would adding a favorite sausage or some crumbled bacon on top, if you love crisp bacon.

1½ cups dried cannellini beans (see cook's note)

2 tablespoons olive oil

1 onion, diced

4 garlic cloves, finely minced

1 whole leek, trimmed, cut lengthwise, rinsed and sliced (about 1½ cups)

2 celery stalks, diced (about 1 cup)

3 carrots, peeled and diced (about 2 cups)

8 cups water or chicken stock

1 large Parmesan rind

2 teaspoons fresh rosemary, chopped

2 teaspoons fresh thyme, chopped

5 cups kale (1 small bunch, stripped from stalk, cut into ribbons and rinsed)

Salt

1. Put the dried beans in a soup pot and fill with water. Bring to a boil, boil for 1 minute, then turn the heat off, cover, and let the beans soak for 1 hour. (Or you can soak beans in a bowl on the counter overnight and avoid this quick-soaking step.) Discard the soaking water.

2. In a soup pot, sauté the onion in the olive oil over medium heat for 5 minutes. Add the garlic, leek, celery and carrots and sauté for another minute or two, until the garlic is fragrant. Add the 8 cups of water, the Parmesan rind to give the soup additional flavor, and the soaked beans and bring to a boil. While it's coming up to a boil, add the rosemary and thyme to the soup. Simmer, covered, for 45 to 55 minutes, until the beans are cooked. Some beans tend to be older, and take longer to cook. Hold off on adding salt until the beans are cooked.

3. After 45 to 55 minutes, or whenever the beans are cooked, add the kale and salt to taste and simmer for an additional 10 minutes, until the kale is very tender. Taste again, and add salt to taste until the flavors shine through.

Cook's Note: Using 3 cups of canned beans (two cans) is also an option. When I made it for friends one day, using canned beans, they all enjoyed the soup, but I wasn't as impressed with the overall flavor. The taste of the canned beans isn't as delectable as fresh cooked, so it is generally worth that one extra step of soaking and cooking the beans in the soup.

Broth with Mini Meatballs, Kale and Cabbage

I never tire of this satisfying soup of mini meatballs in a chicken broth mingled with mellow greens, topped off with Parmesan. It's a good one to serve guests with a salad (followed by a dessert) to make the meal. Baking the meatballs in the oven makes the whole job easier.

MEATBALLS

- ¾ pound ground beef
- ⅓ cup panko bread crumbs or any fresh bread crumbs (crumbed in a food processor)
- ¼ cup water
- ⅓ cup grated Parmesan cheese
- 1 garlic clove, finely minced
- ½ teaspoon dried oregano
- 2 tablespoons minced fresh parsley
- ¾ teaspoon kosher salt
- ¼ teaspoon freshly ground black pepper

SOUP

- 2 tablespoons olive oil
- 1 large onion, diced (about 2 cups)
- 2 garlic cloves, minced
- 2 carrots, peeled, cut in half lengthwise, and sliced into half-moons
- 2½ teaspoons kosher salt, divided
- 8 cups chicken stock, preferably homemade
- 3 cups kale (stripped from stalk, thinly sliced and rinsed)
- 2 cups savoy cabbage, cored and thinly sliced (see cook's note)
- Freshly ground black pepper
- Parmigiano-Reggiano cheese, grated

1. Make the meatballs: Mix the ground beef, panko, water, Parmesan, garlic, oregano, parsley, salt and pepper together in a bowl. Roll into balls about 1 inch in diameter and place on a baking sheet. Preheat the oven to 375°F.

2. Make the soup: Heat the olive oil in a thick-bottomed soup pot over medium heat. Sauté the onion for about 10 minutes, until golden, stirring often and scraping the bottom of the pot to prevent sticking. Add the garlic and cook for another minute over low heat. Add the chicken stock, carrots and 1 teaspoon of salt and bring to a boil. Add the kale and savoy cabbage, lower the heat to a simmer, cover, and cook for about 15 minutes.

3. While the soup is simmering, bake the meatballs for about 12 minutes (they don't brown as much in the oven as they would sautéed in a pan, but that's okay). Remove from the oven and add to the soup, simmering for about 5 minutes to meld the flavors.

4. Taste the soup and add more salt, if needed, and a few grinds of black pepper. Ladle into soup bowls. Pass the cheese at the table.

Cook's Note: Savoy cabbage is the crinkly green cabbage, a bit milder than regular green cabbage. If savoy cabbage is not available, use green cabbage or chopped escarole.

Variation: Add cheese tortellini to the soup.

THE KALE CHRONICLES

Kale and Soups

Not that I want to, but if I had to pick a category where kale shines extraordinarily, it would be in soups.

If you know someone that shies away from kale, serve a kale soup, or soup with kale. There are so many good ones to choose from.

In a soup, kale's large tough leaves melt away; its flavor mellows. There's little of the chewiness or boldness that people can dislike. Kale becomes one with one of our favorite comfort foods. Kale adds even more nutrition (and color) to a dish typically chock-full of vegetables and other wholesome ingredients.

Kale soup often is synonymous with the Portuguese kale soups, migrating to the United States early on with early fishermen and whalers and later with emigrants who brought kale seeds and traditional holidays like the Feast of the Holy Ghost.

Portuguese Americans often continued to celebrate their Feast of the Holy Ghost when they came to the United States, according to Ana Ortins, a Massachusetts chef and instructor who wrote about her heritage in *Portuguese Homestyle Cooking*. Their feast concludes the Easter season, and pays homage to the Holy Ghost called upon in history in times of need. It revolves around a meal that most always includes *sopa do Espirito Santo* (Holy Ghost soup), followed by a Mass and procession.

So many variations of the soup itself depend upon regional influences, but they most always feature greens of kale or cabbage or both. The Portuguese-American Club on Martha's Vineyard makes a huge batch of its Holy Ghost Soup each year. It's a heady combination of whole chuck roast simmering in beef broth, with garlic, onions, potatoes, savory cabbage, kale, linguica sausage and tomatoes. On Martha's Vineyard, you'll also find kale soup sold at the fish market, restaurants, and island dining tables, and on the Steamship Authority boats sailing back and forth between the island and the mainland.

But kale also fits so easily in traditional Italian soups, Asian broths, and with white beans, lentils and chickpeas. Adding the kale is as easy as slicing up the leaves or roughly chopping, and tossing them into the soup with last ten to fifteen minutes of simmering. I love the bright green of the kale as it first hits hot water. For this reason, I occasionally precook the kale in boiling water for four to five minutes, and then add it to the soup at the end just to keep this brightness. The flavor seems similar treated both ways.

Kale has a natural affinity to chicken and beef broth. One of the soups I never tire of combines a homemade chicken broth with mini meatballs (made with beef or turkey) onions, kale and cabbage finished off with a spoonful of Parmesan. Now, I can't even imagine my regular chicken noodle soups without kale.

If you are vegetarian, vegetable and bean soups with kale are equally as good. The kale and farro soup flavored with Parmesan rinds is another all-time favorite. I've even experimented using crispy kale as a soup garnish, for the contrasting textures. It worked just fine with my bourbon, apple and butternut squash soup (also vegetarian) topped with roasted crispy kale, pumpkin seeds and cranberries.

I thought I was finished with the soup section of the book when my friend Laura Roosevelt called with another idea: tortilla soup with shrimp and kale. Laura had added kale and hominy to her version of a tortilla soup: using shrimp rather than chicken, and flavored with garlic, spicy chipotle peppers and lime juice. She topped it with an avocado and tomato salsa, and won raves from her family and guests, which prompted the call to me. "I just love that it's a whole meal in one," she said.

With a kale soup, all you need is a salad for a deeply satisfying meal.

Bourbon Apple Butternut Soup with Roasted Kale and Pumpkin Seeds

SERVES 6

The combination of kale and butternut is a good one, especially enhanced with apples and a hint of bourbon. I had planned to add some cream, but happily, none was needed. The finishing touch is crispy kale roasted with pumpkin seeds and fresh cranberries, which all gives a crunchy, tart contrast to the smooth, pureed soup.

- 2 tablespoons butter
- 1 onion, diced
- 5 cups peeled, seeded, and diced butternut squash (large dice) (from 1 medium-size butternut squash)
- 2 carrots, peeled and cut into rounds (about 1½ cups)
- 1 whole leek, all parts, cut in half lengthwise, rinsed and sliced (a little over 2 cups)
- 2 garlic cloves, minced
- 1 teaspoon finely minced fresh ginger
- ⅓ cup bourbon whiskey

- 5 cups water
- 2 tart apples, peeled, cored and cut in half or into quarters
- 1–2 teaspoons kosher salt, divided
  Freshly ground black pepper
- ½ bunch kale, stripped from stalk, chopped into bite-size pieces and rinsed (about 3 cups)
- 1 tablespoon olive oil
- ½ cup pumpkin seeds
- ¼ cup fresh cranberries

1. Melt the butter in a soup pot and sauté the onion for about 5 minutes. Add the squash, carrots and leek and sauté on medium to medium-high heat for about 10 minutes, stirring often to cook all sides of the squash. Add the garlic and ginger and sauté for about 30 additional seconds, until fragrant.

2. Turn up the heat a bit and add the bourbon, and let the alcohol cook off, about 1 minute. Add the water, apples and 1 teaspoon of the salt, bring to a boil, then lower the heat to a simmer, and cook covered, for about 20 minutes, or until the squash and carrots are easily pierced with a fork. Let cool for 5 or so minutes before blending.

3. Process the soup, in batches, in a blender until smooth and creamy, or use an immersion blender to puree. (Take care when blending a hot soup by filling the container only two-thirds full, placing a kitchen towel over the blender top, and blending from low to high speed.) If the soup is too thick, add some water to thin it a bit. Taste for seasoning and add more salt by the pinches, until really flavorful. Add a few grinds of pepper.

4. Preheat the oven to 350°F while the soup is cooking, and roast the kale. Place the pieces of kale on the baking sheet. Add the olive oil and knead into the kale. Sprinkle with salt and bake for 15 to 20 minutes, or until crispy, but not browned, stirring a few times. When the kale is done, or on another baking sheet, place the pumpkin seeds, seasoned with a pinch or two of salt, and the cranberries, and roast until the seeds are roasted and the cranberries are softened somewhat, 6 to 7 minutes.

5. Ladle into bowls, and top each with the garnish of about 2 tablespoons of the oven-roasted kale (breaking apart if needed), some of the pumpkin seeds, and three or four roasted cranberries. Place any remaining toppings in bowls at the table for people to replenish or munch on.

Variation: Instead of a crispy topping, you can braise the kale and add it directly to the soup. While soup is cooking, bring 4 cups of water to a boil in a sauté pan with a lid and boil 4 cups of chopped kale for 4 to 5 minutes, until tender. Set aside to cool. Once cool, squeeze gently to remove any excess water and break the clumps apart slightly. Stir the kale into the creamy, blended butternut soup. Ladle into bowls and add a few grinds of pepper.

Kale, Bean and Vegetable Soup

This is a quick-cooking soup ready in less than 45 minutes to make use of fall garden or farmers' market vegetables, including your kale. I enjoy the bright green hue of kale cooked separately in this soup. To skip that extra step, add kale directly to soup after it's simmered for 10 minutes.

2 tablespoons olive oil

1 onion, diced

1 whole leek, cut in half lengthwise, rinsed, and sliced

2 cups peeled, seeded, and diced butternut squash (¾-inch dice)

4 carrots, diced (about 1½ cups)

2 celery stalks, diced

3 garlic cloves, finely minced

2 teaspoons chili powder

2 teaspoons dried oregano

6 cups water

Salt

1 (14-ounce) can diced tomatoes, with juices, or 1 cup roasted fresh tomatoes

5 cups kale (about 1 small bunch), stripped from stalk, cut into bite-size pieces and rinsed)

1 (15-ounce) can kidney beans, drained and rinsed

Freshly ground black pepper

1. In a soup pot, sauté the onion in the olive oil for 5 minutes. Add the leek, butternut squash, carrots, celery and garlic and sauté until the leek is wilted, 8 to 10 minutes, stirring often. Add the chili powder and oregano and cook, stirring, for 1 to 2 minutes, until fragrant.

2. Add the water, a few pinches of salt and the tomatoes. Bring to a boil, then lower the heat and simmer, partially covered, for about 20 minutes, until the vegetables are cooked, but not falling apart.

3. Meanwhile, bring 3 cups of water to a boil in a medium-size saucepan and cook the kale, covered, in the boiling water for 5 minutes. Drain, and add to the soup, along with the beans. Season with additional salt, until the flavors pop, and pepper.

Beef, Mushroom and Kale Soup

This beef soup takes a bit longer to cook than other soups in this book, but the flavor and texture make it unbeatable. Chuck roast makes the most flavorful, tender cuts, and though it's a pain to cut up, I think you'll find it worth the effort. Avoid precut stew meat, which is often different cuts that might not cook up as tenderly as the chuck does. If there is extra soup, it freezes well.

1 (2-pound) piece of chuck roast

2 tablespoons olive oil, divided

2 onions, diced (about 2 cups)

3 garlic cloves, finely minced

½ cup red wine

8 cups chicken stock

¼ cup dried mushrooms (porcini, mixed mushrooms or other), rinsed to remove any grit

4 carrots, peeled and diced (2 to 3 cups)

2 parsnips, peeled and diced (about 1½ cups), or 1 small celery root, peeled and diced

1 (14-ounce) can diced tomatoes, with juices

4 cups kale (about ½ bunch, stripped from stalk, cut into bite-size pieces and rinsed)

½ cup farro, rinsed

2 teaspoons fresh thyme, or 1 teaspoon dried
Kosher salt

2 cups sliced mushrooms (optional)
Freshly ground black pepper

1. Cut the beef into similarly sized pieces, smaller that you would cut them for a stew, ¾ to 1 inch across. Cut away any solid fat as you go. Heat 1 tablespoon of the olive oil in a thick-bottomed soup pot on medium-high heat, and sauté the beef cubes in two batches so the pieces brown nicely, 5 to 6 minutes per batch. Remove from the pot and set aside.

2. Sauté the onions for 4 to 5 minutes, then add the garlic and cook for 1 minute, stirring often. Add the wine and scrape up any brown bits. Add the chicken stock and beef and bring to a boil. Skim off any foam that rises to the top, lower the heat to low, and simmer, partially covered, for 40 minutes. Check every once in a while to make sure the water is simmering gently, not boiling.

3. Meanwhile, boil 2 cups of water and pour over the dried mushrooms. Set aside.

4. After 40 minutes, add the carrots, parsnips, tomatoes, kale, farro, thyme, and 1 teaspoon of salt to the soup. Chop the soaked mushrooms fairly small and add, along with the soaking water (but watch for any grit at the bottom of the water). Bring to a boil again, then lower the heat and simmer, partially covered, for another 40 to 50 minutes, or until the beef is fork tender and the farro is cooked. Again, cook at a gentle simmer, not a full boil.

5. During this time, slice and sauté the fresh mushrooms, if using, in a skillet, in the remaining olive oil. Add the sautéed mushrooms to the soup.

6. Season with additional salt and pepper to taste. Add additional water, if needed, or if the soups thicken as it sits.

Lentil, Kale and Vegetable Soup

This soup is chock-full of colorful vegetables, dark leafy kale, protein in the form of the lentils, and a few spices to add to the flavor. French green lentils, also called du Puy, are smaller than the brown lentils, cook quicker and hold their shape to give this lentil soup a nice appearance for once.

2	tablespoons olive oil
1	medium-size onion, diced
1	large (or 2 small or medium-size) whole leek, trimmed, cut in half lengthwise, rinsed and sliced crosswise (2 to 3 cups)
2	medium-size garlic cloves, finely minced
1	teaspoon fresh rosemary, chopped
1	teaspoon fresh thyme, chopped
1	teaspoon dried oregano
1	tablespoon tomato paste
9	cups water
2–3	carrots, peeled and diced (1½ to 2 cups)
1½	cups peeled and diced celery root, or 2 celery stalks, diced
2	cups peeled, seeded, and diced butternut squash (¾-inch dice), or 2 cups chopped turnip (from 1 turnip)
¾	cup French green lentils (du Puy), picked through and rinsed
1	(14-ounce) can diced tomatoes, with juices
1	bunch lacinato (dinosaur) kale (stripped from stalk, chopped or sliced and rinsed (about 5 cups)
1	teaspoon kosher salt, or more to taste

1. Heat the olive oil in a heavy-bottomed soup pot on medium heat. Add the onion and sauté over medium heat for 6 minutes; add the leek and cook for an additional 5 to 6 minutes, stirring often. Add the garlic and herbs and cook for 1 minute. Stir in the tomato paste.

2. Add the water and the carrots, celery root, squash, and lentils. Bring to a boil, then simmer, partially covered, for about 25 minutes. Add the tomatoes and their juices and the kale. Again, bring to a boil, partially cover, and then lower the heat. Simmer for 15 to 20 minutes, or until the lentils and kale are tender. Add the salt, then taste to see whether additional salt is needed.

Main Dishes

Chicken and Kale Dinner Salad with Cilantro–Lime Vinaigrette

Dinner salads topped with a variety chopped vegetables, prepared fish or chicken and a delicious cheese are a savior for nights you can't pull together a cooked dinner, but still want to serve something healthy. In this dish, Mexican flavors of cilantro, lime and chiles flavor chicken, avocado, tomatoes and red onion. Arrange the colorful components in strips or groupings on a platter over the baby kale so people can serve themselves.

5 cups baby kale (longer stems removed, rinsed and dried)	1 ear fresh corn, kernels removed (see cook's note)
2 cups cooked, shredded or diced chicken breast (See page 46 for an easy way to roast chicken.)	2 just-ripe avocados, pitted and diced or sliced
1½ cups queso fresco or feta cheese	2 tomatoes, diced, or ½ pint cherry tomatoes, quartered
1 cup canned black beans, drained and rinsed	½ red onion, slivered
	Salt

CILANTRO-LIME VINAIGRETTE

3 tablespoons fresh lime juice	½ cup olive oil
1–2 garlic cloves, finely minced	½ teaspoon salt
½ cup lightly packed fresh cilantro leaves	

1. Lay the baby kale on large oval or rectangular platter: top with the chicken, cheese, black beans, corn, avocados, tomatoes and red onion. Sprinkle the chicken and vegetables with a pinch or two of salt.

2. Make the vinaigrette: In a blender or food processor, combine the lime juice, garlic, cilantro, olive oil and salt. Blend or process until the ingredients are incorporated. Serve the dressing on the side to pass around. Use immediately.

Cook's Note: Fresh summer corn, served raw in a salad with a dressing, is delicious. If you prefer to cook the corn, steam for 2 or 3 minutes, cool under cold water and drain well. If you want to do all ahead, put the dressing ingredients into the blender jar and place the blender jar in the fridge. When ready to serve, blend the dressing and pass at the table. This ensures an appealing bright green dressing.

Steak, Tomato and Baby Kale

An easy dinner when you don't have much time. Balsamic vinegar is heated and reduced to flavor both the steak and baby kale greens.

2	rib eye or New York strip steaks (about ½ pound each)
	Salt and freshly ground black pepper
1	tablespoon olive oil, plus more for steak
½	cup balsamic vinegar
2	teaspoons pure maple syrup
4–6	cups baby kale (stemmed, rinsed and dried)
2	tomatoes, diced, or 1 pint cherry tomatoes, halved

1. Heat a grill, grill pan or regular thick-bottomed skillet, such as cast-iron, over high heat. Season the steaks with salt and pepper on both sides. Heat a film of olive oil and sear the steaks on high heat for 2 to 3 minutes. Lower the heat to medium and cook for another 2 minutes, until a nice crust forms. Use a pair of tongs to turn the steaks over, then repeat the process. When the steaks are done (125° to 130°F for medium rare), let them rest for at least 5 minutes before slicing.

2. While steaks are being cooked, bring the balsamic vinegar to a boil in a small saucepan. Add the maple syrup and simmer, uncovered, until thickened and reduced to ¼ to ⅓ cup, 6 to 7 minutes.

3. Place the kale and tomatoes on a platter. Drizzle the 1 tablespoon of olive oil and sprinkle a pinch of salt over the vegetables and mix gently with tongs. Slice the steaks and place on top. Drizzle the steaks and kale with the desired amount of the vinegar mixture hot off the stove. (You will probably have some of the mixture left over.) Season with some additional black pepper, if desired.

Kale Crostata with Caramelized Acorn Squash and Onions

SERVES 4 AS A MAIN COURSE, 6 TO 8 AS AN APPETIZER OR SIDE

Heather Milliman is a Dover, New Hampshire–based food stylist, pastry chef, recipe developer and former culinary instructor at Stonewall Kitchen Cooking School in Maine, where we have taught classes together. She created this rustic, yet sophisticated and delicious kale tart, and says this about the results: "There is something so wonderful about pulling this from the oven. Its crust is flaky and tender, enveloping the rich flavors of caramelized vegetables, the simple earthiness of the greens and the cheese."

2 tablespoons butter, divided

2 tablespoons olive oil

1 medium-size acorn squash, halved, seeded, cut into ½-inch thick slices (1½ to 2 pounds)

1 medium-size sweet onion, sliced in half lengthwise, then into thin half-moons

1 tablespoon fresh sage, minced

1 teaspoon fresh thyme, chopped

½ teaspoon fresh rosemary, minced

   Kosher salt and freshly ground black pepper

¼ teaspoon freshly grated nutmeg

⅓ cup dry sherry

¼ cup heavy cream

2 tablespoons tomato paste

2 cups small, tender kale (stripped from stalk, cut into a fine shred and rinsed)

1 sheet frozen puff pastry, thawed

½ cup each grated pecorino and fontina cheeses, combined

1 egg beaten lightly with 2 tablespoons water

   Cornmeal, for dusting work surface

1. Preheat the oven to 400°F.

2. Melt 2 teaspoons of the butter in large, heavy skillet over medium heat; add 1 tablespoon of the olive oil. Add half of the squash slices. Cook until caramelized on both sides and fork tender, about 8 minutes per side. Transfer the squash slices to a rimmed baking sheet. Repeat with the remaining butter, oil and squash. When finished, allow the squash to cool and gently remove the skins.

3. Place the onion in the same skillet and cook over medium heat until wilted and caramelized, about 15 minutes. Add the herbs, nutmeg, sherry, cream, tomato paste and kale and simmer until thickened and the kale is wilted. Season to taste with salt and pepper.

4. Roll out the pastry dough to between ⅛ and ¼ inch in thickness (in a rectangular or rounded shape) on a floured surface and place it on a parchment paper–lined baking sheet. Place ½ cup of the mixed cheeses on the pastry, leaving a margin of about 2 inches around the edge, then place the squash on top of the cheese and spoon the kale mixture on top. Top with the remaining cheese mixture and fold the edges of the dough up over the filling by about an inch to create a rustic tart. Brush with egg wash.

5. Bake for 20 to 30 minutes. Allow to cool slightly. Slice into wedges and serve.

Cook's Note: One of the testers, who enjoyed the crostata and made it several times afterward, said she also substituted butternut squash—peeled, seeded and cut into ½-inch-thick rounds, then strips, which will be of varying lengths.

Kale Cioppino

We live on the island of Martha's Vineyard, where shellfish and striped bass are plentiful, and friends like Dana Knowlton regularly drop quahogs of all sizes on our porch. Dana's wife, Liz, thought a cioppino-like fish stew with herbs, tomato and a bit of stock would be a perfect base for braising kale and nestling clams, mussels and a fresh-caught fish. It is! This is an easy dish, but good enough for company along with chilled white wine and fresh bread or garlic bread. (It's good with just mussels and fish as well.)

- 3 tablespoons olive oil, divided
- 1 tablespoon butter
- 1 *whole* leek, trimmed, cut in half lengthwise and sliced (about 2 cups)
- 3 tablespoons finely minced garlic, divided
- ¼–½ teaspoon red pepper flakes
- ½ cup white wine
- 1½ cups chicken stock, clam juice or water
- 1 (28-ounce) can diced tomatoes, with juices
- 1 teaspoon dried oregano
- 1 teaspoon fresh thyme (or ½ teaspoon dried)
- ½ teaspoon salt
- 3 cups Italian kale (stripped from stalk, cut or sliced into fairly small bite-size pieces and rinsed)
- ½ cup water
- 12 cherrystone clams, scrubbed well
- 18 mussels, rinsed, any "beards" removed
- 1 pound striped bass, halibut or cod, cut into uniform cubes, 1 to 1½ inches across
  Lemon wedges

1. Sauté the leek in 2 tablespoons of the olive oil and the butter on medium heat until soft, 5 to 6 minutes. Add 2 tablespoons of the garlic and the red pepper flakes, and stir for another 30 seconds or so more, until fragrant. Turn up the heat, add the wine and boil for a minute or two. Add the stock, tomatoes, herbs, two pinches of salt and the kale and bring to a boil. Simmer, covered, on medium-low heat for 10 minutes.

2. While the kale is cooking, heat the remaining tablespoon of oil in a wide skillet with a lid, add the remaining tablespoon of garlic and cook until sizzling, 30 seconds. Add the water and bring to a boil. Add the cherrystones, cover, and cook on high heat until the clams open, 7 to 9 minutes.

3. Add the mussels and nestle the bass in the kale mixture. Cover, and simmer on medium heat until the mussels are open, 3 to 4 minutes more. Try not to stir too much, to keep the fish from breaking up.

4. To serve: Carefully spoon a few mussels, clams and fish into the middle of a wide soup or pasta bowl; spoon the sauce of leeks, tomatoes and kale around the seafood. Add a lemon wedge.

Crispy Herbed Fish Baked over Kale

An easy preparation for a weeknight, but can be prepped ahead for company. It calls for either Italian or Red Russian kale, either of which melts down better than curly kale and fit under the fish, which is then baked with herbs, butter and bread crumbs. The squeeze of lemon juice at the end flavors both the fish and the kale.

¾ pound Italian, Red Russian kale or tender young kale, stripped from stalk, cut into bite-size pieces and rinsed (1 bunch, or 5 to 6 cups)

1 tablespoon plus 2 teaspoons olive oil, divided

3 garlic cloves, finely minced (about 1½ teaspoons)
Kosher salt and freshly ground black pepper

4 pieces of flounder or sole (about 1½ pounds total)

3 tablespoons butter, softened or melted

3 tablespoons fresh herbs or a combination (parsley, chives and/or dill)
Zest of 1 lemon (2 to 3 teaspoons)

⅓ cup panko bread crumbs

1 lemon, cut into wedges

1. Preheat the oven to 375°F. Precook the kale in about 4 cups of water, in a wide covered sauté pan or soup pot, for 4 to 6 minutes, until tender. Strain in a colander and shake to release the steam. Wipe the pan, and add the tablespoon of olive oil and garlic. Sauté over low heat until the garlic is fragrant, about 30 seconds or so. Turn off the heat, add the kale and two pinches of salt and mix well off the heat.

2. Place the kale in a lasagne-size baking dish, in four spots where the fish will lay on top of it (or in four individual baking dishes), and place a piece of fish on top. Season the fish with salt and pepper. Smear butter over each piece. Top the fish with the herbs and lemon zest. In a small bowl, mix the bread crumbs with the remaining 2 teaspoons of olive oil. Top the fish with the bread crumb mixture.

3. Place the pan in the oven. Smaller, thinner pieces of fish may be done in 7 to 12 minutes; larger, thicker pieces can take 11 to 13 minutes. Broil at the end to brown and crisp the bread crumbs, if needed. Before serving, squeeze some lemon juice over each piece.

4. With a long spatula, carefully lift under the kale and place the kale and its fish on a plate. Pour any remaining pan juices over the fish.

Cook's Notes:
- Serve with a vegetable or salad of a different color, such as baked squash in the fall, roasted carrots or carrot salad in the spring, or a tomato salad in summer.
- A colleague who tested this recipe had a good idea for preparing this in a cast-iron pan. She halved the recipe to serve two, cooked the kale in a cast-iron pan—and baked the fish on top in the same pan.

Turkey and Kale Meat Loaf

Kale and other vegetables provide the moisture that is often lacking in a turkey meat loaf. The kale is minced. You can also finely chop the onion, celery and carrot together in a food processor and then squeeze out any additional moisture. If dark meat ground turkey is available, a combination of half dark and half white meat works well. Serve with the Mashed Potatoes with Kale side dish (page 165) for a delicious dinner.

MEAT LOAF

- 3 large kale leaves, stripped from stalk, chopped into small bits and rinsed (1½ cups)
- 2 teaspoons olive oil
- 1½ pounds natural ground turkey breast (half dark meat; half white meat, if available)
- ½ cup finely minced onion
- ½ cup panko, bread crumbs or quick oats
- 1 egg
- ½ cup minced celery

- ½ cup shredded carrot
- ½ teaspoon minced fresh garlic
- ⅓ cup milk or plain yogurt
  Freshly ground black pepper
- ¾ teaspoon kosher salt
- ½ teaspoon dried thyme
- ½ teaspoon dried oregano
- 1 tablespoon Dijon mustard

TOPPING

- ½ cup ketchup
- 2 teaspoons brown sugar or pure maple syrup

- 1 teaspoon mustard
- 1 teaspoon molasses or barbecue sauce

1. Make the meat loaf: Place the kale in a bowl and sprinkle with the olive oil. With your hands, massage the kale for 2 to 3 minutes, until the kale is reduced a little in volume and bright green. (You can also chop the kale again if pieces are still too large.)

2. Preheat the oven to 350°F. Oil a 9- or 10-inch glass pie plate and set aside.

3. In a medium-size bowl, mix all the meat loaf ingredients together, including the kale. Pat the mixture into the pie plate.

4. Make the topping: Mix the ketchup, brown sugar, mustard and molasses together in a small bowl. Spread on top of the turkey loaf and bake for 40 to 45 minutes, or until the meat begins to pull away from the sides of the pan. Allow to rest for 5 minutes before cutting into wedges.

Fast and Fresh Kale Dinner Salad with Salmon and Prosciutto

When I first made this warm-weather salad for a casual outdoor gathering with family and guests, everyone commented on the appeal of the dish they eagerly sampled. But the true benefit for the cook is the ease of putting this together—minimal effort with a big payoff because the salmon and prosciutto are ready to go. It's best to use tender baby kale here—not torn up regular kale.

4–5 cups baby kale (stemmed, rinsed and dried)

1 tomato, cut into chunks, or 1 cup cherry tomatoes, halved

1 cucumber, peeled to leave thin strips of dark green, cut in half lengthwise and sliced

1 just-ripe avocado, pitted and sliced

4 radishes, halved and thinly sliced

1 (8- to 12-ounce) package chunky smoked salmon or smoked black pepper salmon fillets (not sliced smoked salmon, see cook's note)

8–12 slices of prosciutto, gently rolled

8 ounces fresh mozzarella, sliced, or small mozzarella balls, halved

3 hard-boiled eggs, quartered (see page 46 for best method to hard-boil)

LEMON MUSTARD DRESSING

3 tablespoons fresh lemon juice

2 teaspoons Dijon mustard

1 teaspoon honey or other sweetener

1 garlic clove, finely minced

½ cup olive oil

1 tablespoon chopped fresh herb, such as basil, parsley, oregano or chives, or 1 teaspoon dried oregano

½ teaspoon kosher salt

Freshly ground black pepper

1. Place the kale in a large, wide bowl, or platter, with enough room to show off the toppings. In similar groupings, place the tomatoes, cucumber, avocado and radishes on top. Break the smoked salmon fillet into medium-size to large chunks. Place the rolled prosciutto on top, along with slices or pieces of mozzarella, and the egg quarters.

2. Make the dressing: Whisk together the lemon juice, Dijon, honey, garlic, olive oil, herbs, salt and pepper in a mason jar or salad jar. Pass the dressing at the table, and let each guest spoon or pour on their own. If the dressing separates, remind your diners to whisk or shake before spooning over their salad. If you make ahead, save the avocado and slice at serving time.

Cook's Note: The packages of salmon fillets at my local fish market are smoked, moist and tasty, sometimes coming with cracked pepper on top, which looks appealing. I have seen pieces in markets that look drier and might not be as appealing. The salmon fillets I use are whole pieces of salmon, not to be confused the thinly sliced smoked salmon. However, if the chunkier fillets are unavailable, these could be rolled and substituted. Or you could grill or bake your own salmon and serve at room temperature.

THE KALE CHRONICLES

How to Organize a Kale Fest in Your Area

I often stop by Chilmark's Mermaid Farm to pick up the vegetables, yogurt or cheese. Allen is the dairy guy—raising the cows and making the most creamy delicious yogurt on the island (or anywhere). Caitlin grows the vegetables. She specializes in heirloom tomatoes, but she is always experimenting with one thing or another. I've seen a fig tree growing in the hoop house or ginger plants for sale at the very small self-serve stand. Sometimes, I'll find freshly picked, nonsprayed raspberries or strawberries—you never know what food treasure you might find here.

In 2011, with her friend Dan Sternbach, Caitlin had planted two or three giant patches of kale, along with several patches that would winter over inside hoop houses. We're talking hundreds of kale plants—and some kale varieties I had never seen.

"Let's have a kale festival," she said to me out of the blue one day.

This was two years before I would embark on writing a whole book dedicated to kale.

"Sure," I said.

This was mid-November, and we needed to schedule the event soon while we could still have the event outside. We settled on December 4, giving us about two weeks to pull it off—not much time to create posters, get the word out, find a few volunteers and so forth . . .

We wanted the festival to be fun, and we embraced every crazy idea we came up with. We'd have a kale brunch, have kids judge the dishes and crown a kale king and a kale queen. We wanted it to be free, so expenses needed to be kept to a minimum. We had plenty of the raw ingredients, a savings right there. It turned out that Jackee Foster, the cheese maker at the farm at the time, was a closet graphic designer. She created the "Hail, King Kale" poster with shades of green, kale trivia and an outline of the day's events.

The prime motivation for me: I wanted people to learn about kale, especially good ways to prepare it. What was reverberating in my mind was the afternoon I spent six months earlier at another Vineyard farm, collecting interviews and color for a story on the island's CSA. That afternoon, I was very surprised to witness people giving away their kale, trading it for other vegetables or just not even taking it. They either didn't like kale they said or didn't know how to cook it. I was confident, with a little coaching and a good basic recipe or two, I could change their minds. (I even took some e-mails addresses that day and sent off favorite kale recipes.)

So on my list for the festival would be free cooking demos throughout the day. I knew exactly who to turn to. Susie Middleton, a former editor of *Fine Cooking* and author of *Fast, Fresh & Green*, among other vegetable-centric cookbooks, happily volunteered to share her expertise, as did Jan Buhrman, one of the island's top caterers and a kale aficionado, as well as a Slow Food board member. I also tapped my close friend Berni Cormie, owner of Herring Run Kitchen catering.

The location for some of the "classes" was a hoop house in the fields. We hauled in a few rows of hay bales to sit on and we set up a table with a tablecloth for the instructors. It was so cozy, and fitting. We could get about twenty people in there at a time to watch the demos and sample kale dishes.

The other class setting was a large open shed, also set up with hay bales with some long planks on top, and several long tables. After the two scheduled demos here, we would turn this area into the spot for the kale potluck. We had a table set aside for the potluck dishes, and had lined up some kids who were involved with school gardens to judge. (In our prepublicity about the event, we mentioned we would leave tried-and-true kale recipe cards at the farm stand as well as fall fresh kale for sale, in case people needed ideas of what to bring.) All we needed for the day was decent weather, and attendees.

We were tremendously lucky that the day turned out to be a sunny and warm day for a December Sunday. About 75 to 80 people showed up. And as at any event on a farm, families wandered around, visiting the baby calves, communing with the Zen-like sheep and avoiding the two annoying Aflac-like ducks that preside on the grounds. The demos were packed and plenty of kale recipes handed out. Throughout the day, Caitlin and Dan offered tours and informal talks about growing kale, especially during the winter.

We didn't know what might come in the form of kale dishes for the potluck. The cooking instructors agreed to prepare a little extra of their dishes to share, just in case. I made a big batch of Italian kale wedding soup with mini meatballs. But it wasn't necessary. People brought kale casseroles, salads, soups, breads—a long table of kale incarnations. After the judging, we sampled and sat on the hay bales, socializing.

We didn't have a kale queen and king that day, but three queens with winning dishes. Jessica, a lawyer and mother of two, made a kale pizza with caramelized onions and Mermaid Farm feta. Hara, who works at the local marina and is a graduate of the Natural Gourmet Institute, made the most of her Greek heritage with kale spanakopita. Jackee, the cheese maker and poster designer, turns out to be an accomplished cook as well. She made a massaged kale salad with apples, dried cranberries, sunflower seeds and her own handmade farm feta, of course. They wore green crowns and were given kale bouquets. We posted all the recipes on the Slow Food MV website, and I've also included all three in this book.

My best gift came from Caitlin for helping to pull off the island's first ever kale fest. I could pick kale from inside the hoop house all winter long, anytime I wanted. It was like winning green in the lottery.

Spanish Rice, Kale and Chicken

SERVES 4

This is a fast, one-pot chicken and kale meal, using sweet smoked paprika, which infuses the whole dish with flavor. It uses leftover or rotisserie chicken but can also work with tofu or beans. See page 48 for a quick way to roast chicken, if you don't have roasted chicken on hand. A leek is used here rather than an onion because it cooks quickly and is flavorful.

- 2 tablespoons olive oil
- 1 leek, trimmed, rinsed, cut lengthwise and sliced (about 2 cups)
- 2–3 cloves finely minced garlic
- 2 teaspoons smoked sweet paprika (see cook's note)
- 2 teaspoons fresh thyme, or 1 teaspoon dried
- 3 cups water or chicken stock
- 3 cups kale (about ½ bunch, stripped from stalk, cut into bite-size pieces and rinsed)
- 1 (14-ounce) can diced tomatoes, juices drained
- 1½ cups white rice—jasmine, basmati or regular long-grain
- ½ teaspoon salt
- 2 cups diced cooked chicken
- 1½ cups grated Cheddar cheese

1. In a Dutch oven or ovenproof sauté pan with a lid, heat the olive oil and leek over medium heat and sauté for 4 to 5 minutes, until the leek is wilted. Add the garlic and sauté for another 30 seconds. Add the paprika, thyme, water, kale, tomatoes, rice and salt and bring to a boil, stirring often to incorporate the kale, which will shrink. Lower the temperature, cover, and cook on low heat for 12 minutes, until the rice is done. Meanwhile, preheat the oven to 350°F.

2. Test the rice to make sure it's cooked; slightly al dente is fine. If so, add the diced chicken and cheese and stir once to distribute. Bake for 10 minutes, until the chicken is heated and the cheese is melted. Serve immediately.

Cook's Note: Smoked sweet paprika is a nice spice to have on hand for the wonderful smoky flavor it can bring to dishes. I've made this dish with water instead of stock, because the smoked paprika can carry the dish. Please don't use regular smoked paprika or spicy paprika—it will be too hot. Regular paprika won't add the same flavor as the smoked sweet.

Basic Roast Chicken and Kale

One of my favorite and simplest meals to make is roast chicken, with kale and squash. The squash and chicken bake on their own in the oven, and the kale side dish takes about 5 minutes—and usually benefits from an easy pan sauce. The kale is sautéed simply with garlic here, but any one of the kale sides would also work here—kale and raisins and pine nuts, kale and leeks, mashed potatoes and kale, roasted kale and cauliflower.

1 (3½- to 4½-pound) chicken

1 tablespoon olive oil for kale, plus olive oil or softened butter, to rub on chicken

2 tablespoons butter

Kosher salt

2 delicata squashes, cut in half and seeded

Ground cinnamon

Pure maple syrup or brown sugar

1 bunch kale, stripped from stalk, roughly chopped and rinsed (6 to 8 cups)

2 garlic cloves, finely minced

Lemon wedge

All-purpose flour

1 cup water or chicken stock

1. Preheat the oven to 425°F. Rub the chicken with a little olive oil and season generously with salt. Place breast side down on a roasting rack inside a roasting pan. After 30 minutes, turn the chicken over. It will have marks from the rack, but those will disappear as the chicken roasts for an additional 30 minutes or so. After 70 minutes to 1 hour 20 minutes total, insert a thermometer into the thigh (without touching a bone) and remove when it is about 165°F.

2. Place the squash halves, cut side down, on a parchment paper–sheet pan. Place in the oven about 30 minutes before the chicken is done. Bake until soft, but not collapsed, 20 to 25 minutes. When done, add a dab of butter to each one, and season with salt. Place a shake of cinnamon and a little maple syrup in each squash half.

3. Bring to a boil a sauté pan of 4 cups of water and cook the kale, covered, for 4 to 6 minutes. Drain, and shake to release the steam. Wipe out the sauté pan, add 1 tablespoon of olive oil and the garlic and cook on low heat until the garlic is sizzling, about 1 minute. Add back the kale, season with salt, and mix well.

4. Transfer the chicken to a cutting board or dish, cover loosely with foil and let rest for 10 to 15 minutes. To make a pan sauce while the chicken is resting, spoon off any fat. Add a tablespoon of butter and tablespoon of flour to the roasting pan over medium heat (if it's a pan that also goes on the stove). Whisk together as the butter melts, and add up to 1 cup of water or chicken stock, whisking together. Let the sauce bubble; season with salt. Add additional liquid, if needed.

5. Reheat the kale, and put the squash back in the oven to reheat. Slice the chicken, and arrange on a plate with some sauce, kale and squash. Enjoy.

Kale-kopita

Spanakopita is a baked Greek dish made with crackly layers of thin phyllo sheets encasing a mix of feta cheese, greens and fresh herbs. It's a great vehicle for kale, as lunch or dinner with a Greek salad or an appetizer. A flavorful, tangy feta—such as Valbreso French sheep's milk feta or the Greek sheep's and goat's milk combination—along with fresh herbs, such as mint and dill, give this kale-kopita a wonderful flavor. Don't skip this kale dish just because you have never used phyllo—it's not difficult.

2 good-size bunches kale or about 10 cups packed kale, stripped from stalk, chopped into bite-size pieces and rinsed

2 tablespoons olive oil

2 onions, diced (about 2 cups)

2 garlic cloves, finely minced (about 2 teaspoons)
  Kosher salt

2 eggs

1½ cups feta cheese

½ cup cottage cheese

3 tablespoons fresh parsley, dill or mint leaves, or a combination (I especially like to use dill and mint together), chopped

6 tablespoons salted butter, melted, or more if needed

20 (9 x 14-inch) sheets frozen phyllo dough, thawed

1. Bring at least 6 to 8 cups water to a boil in a large skillet with a lid or a wide soup pot. Add the kale, mix with tongs, cover, and boil for 4 to 5 minutes, or until tender. Drain the kale into a colander, and shake several times to let the steam escape. Set aside to cool. Squeeze out any moisture from the kale before using, then break apart and loosen any leaves that clump. Chop again, if the leaves are too big. After squeezing out any additional water from the kale, you should have 3½ to 4 cups of cooked kale.

2. Wipe the skillet dry, and sauté the onions in the olive oil until golden and fully cooked, about 10 minutes. Add the garlic and a few pinches of salt and cook for a minute or two more. Set aside to cool.

3. Place the eggs in a large bowl and whisk well. Crumble the feta cheese into the eggs along with the cottage cheese, onions and herbs. Season the mixture with salt.

4. Preheat the oven to 350°F. Melt the butter. Brush the bottom of a 9 x 12-inch (or similar size) glass baking dish with butter. Place a phyllo sheet in the prepared dish. Use a pastry brush to lightly coat with melted butter. Repeat with nine more sheets of phyllo. Add the kale mixture and spread out evenly. Then top with 10 more sheets, each lightly buttered. With a knife, score the top layer of phyllo into servings to ensure easier cutting of the pieces later. Bake for 40 to 45 minutes, or until golden.

Triangles Variation: Use the same filling to make appetizer-size triangles, or larger triangles. I love the shape and serving size of the larger triangles for lunch or dinner. To do make the larger one, butter three 9 x 12-inch phyllo sheets. Fold them in half. Place about ¼ cup of the kale mixture at one end. Fold up like a flag, and brush the final triangle with a bit of butter and place on the parchment paper–lined baking sheet. Bake at 350°F until golden, 20 to 25 minutes. The triangles can be kept, covered, on their pan in the fridge for one or two days before baking.

Chicken, Carrot and Kale Stir-fry

Kale makes a good substitution and change of pace from broccoli or bok choy in a stir-fry. The color of the red pepper and carrot with the kale is a colorful combination. You can substitute tofu for the chicken to make this a vegetarian dish.

1 cup jasmine or basmati rice

Salt

2–3 tablespoons coconut, peanut or vegetable oil, divided

1 red bell pepper, cored and cut into thin strips

1 large carrot, peeled and cut into matchsticks

4 cups kale (stripped from stalk, chopped into bite-size pieces, and rinsed)

1 whole, boneless skinless chicken breast, cut into thin strips (about 2 cups) (see cook's note)

2 scallions, white and green parts, chopped

2 teaspoons minced garlic

1 tablespoon finely minced fresh ginger

⅛–¼ teaspoon red pepper flakes

GINGER SOY STIR-FRY SAUCE

2 tablespoons rice cooking wine or sherry

3 tablespoons soy sauce

2 tablespoons brown sugar

2 teaspoons cornstarch

1 cup water or chicken stock

1. Make the rice: Combine the rice with 2 cups of water in a saucepan and bring to a boil. Add two pinches of salt, lower the heat to low, cover and simmer for about 12 minutes without disturbing, or until the water is absorbed. Move to another burner and let cool with the cover on for 5 minutes. Set aside.

2. Make the sauce: In a bowl, stir together the rice wine, soy sauce, brown sugar, cornstarch and water.

3. Heat a large heavy skillet or wok over medium-high heat. Heat 1 tablespoon of your oil of choice and stir-fry the red pepper, carrot and kale together for about 3 minutes, tossing with tongs the whole time. Transfer to a platter. Add another 2 teaspoons of oil and the chicken and stir-fry on medium-high heat for another 3 minutes. Don't worry about slightly undercooking the chicken; it will finish in the sauce. The chicken might also stick a bit; use a spatula to toss if it does. Place with the vegetables.

4. Add the remaining 2 teaspoons of oil along with the scallions, garlic, ginger and red pepper flakes and stir-fry for about 30 seconds. Add the sauce, bring to a boil, and then simmer on low heat for 2 to 3 minutes. Add the vegetables and chicken back just to reheat.

5. Place the rice on a serving platter or wide serving bowl. Top with the stir-fry. Serve immediately.

Cook's Note: An easy way to cut chicken into strips is to first remove the tenderloins, and cut away the center cartilage that separates the two cutlets. Then lay the cutlet on the cutting board and, with your knife horizontally to the cutting board, put one hand firmly on top of the chicken breast and carefully cut the chicken breast in half—producing two thinner cutlets. Then take each half cutlet, and cut it into thin strips. Repeat with the other cutlets.

Cider-Braised Kale and Chicken SERVES 4

Chicken, carrots, parsnips and kale are braised in apple cider and stock, thickened slightly. You need your largest skillet with a lid to fit it all in; mine is 13 inches. Serve over mashed potatoes or mixed rice.

6 good-sized bone-in chicken thighs
   Salt and freshly ground black pepper
¼ cup all-purpose flour, for dusting
1 tablespoon olive oil
1 tablespoon butter
1 medium-size onion, thinly sliced
2 teaspoons fresh sage, or ½ teaspoon dried
2 teaspoons fresh thyme, or ½ teaspoon dried
3 carrots, peeled, cut in half lengthwise and sliced
   diagonally into ½-inch pieces (about 1½ cups)
2 medium-size parsnips, peeled, cut in half lengthwise and sliced diagonally into ½-inch pieces (about 1½ cups)
1½ cups apple or hard apple cider
½–1 cup chicken stock
2 tablespoons cider vinegar
   Salt
4 cups kale (stripped from stalk, thinly sliced and rinsed)

1. Rinse the chicken and dry with paper towels. Season the pieces with salt and pepper and dredge in the flour.

2. Heat the olive oil in a large sauté pan with a lid on medium-high heat until sizzling. Add the chicken, skin side down, and brown, about 5 minutes, until the skin is golden. Flip over and brown briefly on the other side. Remove from the pan and set aside briefly. Pour out any fat from the pan.

3. Lower the heat to medium and add the butter and onion; sauté for about 4 minutes, stirring often. Add the sage, thyme, carrots and parsnips and stir constantly for another 2 to 3 minutes. Stir in 2 tablespoons of the flour, then add the apple cider, chicken stock, cider vinegar and a few pinches of salt. Stir until slightly thickened. Add the kale and bring to a boil. When the mixture is boiling and the kale has reduced slightly, add the chicken back in. Lower the heat to low, cover, and cook for about 35 minutes. Check once or twice during the cooking to make sure the liquid is simmering, not boiling. Add the additional stock if needed. Taste for salt.

Mediterranean Dinner Salad with Seared Tuna

These are all ingredients that pair well with tuna for a fast warm-weather dinner salad or a luxurious luncheon dish using baby kale leaves as the healthy base. This can all be plated in advance, with the vinaigrette passed at the table. If you love olives, a different cheese, or prefer canned tuna, make it your own.

1 pound fresh sushi-grade tuna (about 1 medium-size steak)

1 tablespoon dried spice mix, such as Cajun (my favorite) or lemon pepper

1 tablespoon canola or olive oil

6 cups baby kale (longer stems removed, rinsed and dried)

3 hard-boiled eggs, quartered

2 cups cherry tomatoes, halved

1 just-ripe avocado, pitted and sliced

½ red onion, thinly sliced

1 cucumber, peeled and sliced, or 1 red bell pepper, roasted (optional)

1 (15-ounce) can cannellini beans, drained and rinsed

1 cup feta cheese, sheep's milk or Greek feta recommended, crumbled

SUMMER HERB VINAIGRETTE

3 tablespoons fresh lemon juice

1 teaspoon honey

2 teaspoons Dijon mustard

½ cup olive oil

1 garlic clove, minced

2 tablespoons fresh herbs (such as basil, mint, parsley or a combination), or 1 teaspoon dried oregano

Salt and freshly ground black pepper

1. Sear the tuna about an hour before making the salad: Place the spice mix on a plate and dredge the tuna on both sides. Heat a heavy-bottomed or cast-iron sauté pan on medium-high heat, and when hot, pour in the canola oil. Immediately add the tuna and sear on one side, 2 to 3 minutes, until a ¼-inch crust forms. Turn the tuna and sear the other side. (The spice mixture helps the tuna form a good crust). Refrigerate the tuna, uncovered, for about an hour.

2. Make the vinaigrette. Whisk together the lemon juice, honey, Dijon, olive oil, garlic, herbs, and salt and pepper in a mason jar or bowl.

3. Place the baby kale in a large, wide bowl, or platter, with enough room to show off the toppings. Arrange the vegetables over the kale. Use about a tablespoon of the dressing to instantly marinate the drained beans, then place the beans on top of the vegetables. Use a sharp knife to slice the tuna against the grain into thin pieces, about ¼ inch thick, and place on the kale. Crumble the feta and add.

4. Pass the dressing at the table, and let the guests spoon or pour on their own. If the dressing separates, remind your diners to whisk or shake before spooning over their salad.

ACKNOWLEDGMENTS

As creative as you need to be to write a cookbook, there are some recipes I never would have thought of, and so I appreciate the contributions from other kale experts. These other kale dishes and cocktails rounded out the recipes, increasing the variety, for which I'm grateful. Thank you to the following chefs and friends who contributed: Connie Warden, former restaurant owner and chef from St. Albans, Vermont; Chris Fischer, chef at the Beach Plum Restaurant on Martha's Vineyard; Meaghan Sinclair and Harmony Dawn of Booze Époque Bartending Catering Co. in Somerville, Massachusetts; Tamara Weiss, business owner of Midnight Farm on Martha's Vineyard; Quincy Jones, White House chef and valet; Jim Feiner, owner of Feiner Real Estate on Martha's Vineyard; Heather Milliman, a recipe developer and pastry chef from Dover, New Hampshire; Eric Pyenson, of Newton, Massachusetts; Kathy Gunst, cookbook author of South Berwick, Maine; Randi Baird, professional photographer on Martha's Vineyard; Nicole Cabot, private chef of Martha's Vineyard; Rachel Vaughn, private chef of Bozeman, Montana, and Martha's Vineyard; Jackee Foster, cheese maker on Martha's Vineyard; and Jessica Roddy, a Martha's Vineyard lawyer. I got some great ideas from Laura Roosevelt, cookbook author Karen Covey, Julia Kelliher and Christine Redfield.

A very special thanks to Sarah Vail for her invaluable help. Sarah is a close friend, creative cook and huge kale fan. On our weekly walking excursions we talked kale and the many ways it could be used. Without her ideas, some of my favorite recipes would not have not come to be, including the kale latkes and kale spring rolls, among others.

The recipe testing is an important job in making a worthwhile cookbook, with recipes that work. I thoroughly enjoyed the back and forth e-mail conversations with testers and valued their input and suggestions. Testers included Ellen Blue, Sofya Nadelstein, Jessica Roddy, Leslie Gray, Linda London-Thompson, Jean MacRae, Nancy Woods, Pam Redmont, Christine Redmond, Laura Wainwright, Judy Hickey, Pat Kauffman, Laura Roosevelt, Kate Feiffer, Melissa Hackney, Erica DeLorenzo, Kathy and Jim Newman, Linda Doyle Leonard, Barbara Welsh, Patty Zadeh, Liz Knowlton, Liza Thorn Smith, Sue Carroll, Sarah Vail, Robin Nagle, Julia Kelliher and Caren Myers.

I'm grateful to my community of friends and colleagues who so generously offered their support to me in various ways. Friend and cook Hara Dretaki and I spent a night creating an entire Greek menu around kale. Soyfa Nadelstein organized a girls' "Kale and Cocktails" night. I appreciate all who brought dishes as well as tested them. Jessica Roddy opened her house for a kale pizza testing night. Mollie Doyle set me on the right track for getting health information on kale. Cookbook author Susie Middleton gave me the idea for the "Flavors and Foods Kale Loves" list. Thanks also to Deneen McQueen, Megan Sargent, Max King, Jamie Kagliery Stringfellow, Mary Estella, Mary and Sharif Nada, Lynda Shebab and Linda Sacks. I really enjoyed the time that Merrie Nydam spent at our house, smack in the middle of kale testing. Her support meant a lot to me.

Several Vineyard farmers grow lots of kale and allowed us to take photos of their kale fields, along with providing some good growing tips. These include Rusty Gordon of Ghost Island Farm; Debbie Farber of Blackwater Farm; the Athearns of Morning Glory Farm; and Lisa Fisher of Stannard Farms.

Special thanks to Jane Karol, Howard Cooper, Sara and Hope for their love of kale and support of my work.

I love working with Alison Shaw. Her photos always capture the essence and beauty of the dishes and give the readers cause to make the recipes. She is a true artist, who gives 1,000 percent and never ceases to amaze me with her unassuming talent.

As always, my agent, Claire Pelino, has my back.

My son, James, and husband, David, were entirely supportive, including not one complaint when I served them kale for 140 consecutive days. Their only comment was—once—"Where are all the kale dishes with meat?"

MEASUREMENT CONVERSION TABLES

The following tables provide equivalents for U.S., and metric units of measure. Values have been rounded up or down to the nearest whole number.

VOLUME	
U.S.	METRIC
1 teaspoon	5 milliliters
1 tablespoon	15 milliliters
¼ cup	59 milliliters
⅓ cup	79 milliliters
½ cup	118 milliliters
¾ cup	177 milliliters
1 cup	237 milliliters
4 cups (1 quart)	.95 liter
1.06 quarts	1 liter
4 quarts (1 gallon)	3.8 liters

WEIGHT	
OUNCES	GRAMS
½	14
1	28
8	227
12	340
16 (1 pound)	454

INDEX

Note: Page references in *italics* indicate recipe photographs.